Elders Rock!

Don't Just Get Older: Become An Elder

Harvey W. Austin, M.D.

HarveyWAustin@Yahoo.com
601 SE 28th Avenue
Pompano Beach, FL 33062

http://book.eldersrock.com

ISBN-13: 978-0-9965431-0-1
ISBN-10: 0996543104
Library of Congress Control Number: 2015951542
Hagaberry Publishing; Berlin, MD

http://book.eldersrock.com

Table of Contents

Praise for *Elders Rock!*

"The book is simply a brilliant piece of work and I was not able to put it down!" – *Jon Mackler, Chief Strategy Officer*

"*Elders Rock* is the book whose time has come! I am inspired by its wisdom, courage, and humor. Harvey is fearless and unstoppable in his Elderhood. His invitation to us is clear. Read it, be it, do it." – *Dr. Arleen Bump, Former President, Religious Science International, and Senior Pastor, Center for Spiritual Living, Fort Lauderdale, Florida*

"Elder is perhaps *the* major secret of our times." – *Elizabeth Arrott, Author*

"Harvey Austin clearly, cleverly, and compassionately shows us why we and the world need us to graduate into Elderhood, and he provides us with a vibrant and joyful curriculum for doing so." – *Carolyn Baker, Author*

"Dr. Austin has written a significant work on the role of elder in society." – *Alan Mesher, Author*

"Austin skillfully shows how Elders (as distinguished from people who have merely grown old) are necessary for the collective well-being of our world." – *Ron Pevny, Author and Director, Center for Conscious Eldering*

"I am absolutely delighted that you have taken on the monumental project of honoring and resurrecting the idea of Elder in our society and culture." – *David Presler, Cantor*

"Harvey Austin's book is a godsend to anyone who is advancing in years! Not only does he identify his own processes, he makes them available to the reader. And he also has discovered that elders do, indeed, rock! There is a lot more future available to elders than we might have supposed. Austin presents ways to make that future more valuable and interesting than we could have imagined. It doesn't get any better than this!" – *Margaret Stortz, President, United Church of Religious Science, retired ... and rockin' Elder*

"We wholeheartedly embrace your subject, Harvey." – *The Bookswork Team*

"*ELDERS ROCK!* can be your Elder training manual. Use it and rejoice." – *Sam Daley-Harris, Founder, RESULTS and the Center for Citizen Empowerment*

"Your book is a source of Elder wonderment! No other book I have experienced ... couples historical reference with personal experiences and defines the state of elder wisdom in such an enlightening, yet obvious, way." – *Lulu Farrell, Strategic Director, Veterans 4 You*

"Austin makes a clarion call for Western cultures, in particular, to reclaim the lost potential of elder roles in parenting, teaching, mentoring, volunteerism, and intergenerational activities." – *William A. Marjenhoff, retired U.S. Foreign Service Officer*

"This book is packed with nuggets and explosions of valuable life instruction, even for twenty-somethings who are simply Future Elders in Training, whether they know it or not." – *Mary VanMeer, Elder, social media expert, and president of VirtualAssistantGazette.com*

Acknowledgements

I honor and acknowledge my wife, Ellen Tolliver, a most youthful Elder, for providing me the time and space to write this book while she took on, literally, everything else in our life, including spending countless hours editing the early drafts. Your commitment to making a difference in the world and to supporting my well-being has never been and cannot ever be acknowledged sufficiently.

I acknowledge Werner Erhard as the source of transformation in my life and whom I honor as possibly the most influential human being of the last of the twentieth century and the early twenty-first. His not-yet-widely-acclaimed work is brilliant, seminal and transforming.

I acknowledge my parents, Rose Lucy Joyal Austin and Ralph Burrell Austin.

I acknowledge gerontologist and author, William H. Thomas, M.D., for his profound commitment to transforming the care of the Aged in the U.S. Your books and your speaking are eloquent and compelling and I have taken your words and ideas to heart. Bill, I thank you for your permission to quote your writing so extensively.

I acknowledge Dr. Arleen Bump, Senior Pastor of the Center for Spiritual Living, Fort Lauderdale, Florida, and former President, Religious Science International, for being my closest friend and advisor.

Your commitment to a worldview of You AND Me resounds from your pulpit and impacts the future with power and compassion.

I acknowledge certain powerful teachers in my past. I have learned from you what I needed in order to establish the foundation for who I am in the world, without which the writing of this book would not have occurred.

Among these are Randy McNamara, Stewart Esposito, Kelly Townsend, Doug Plette, Barbara Marx Hubbard, Sam Daley-Harris, Joan Holmes, Ken Schatz, Will Richardson, George Weston, Rob Sigal, Brian Poindexter, Jack Gaisford, Dwight Hanna, George Richardson, Ron Friedman, Carole Kammen, Lynnaea Lumbard, Rick Paine, Raz Ingrasci, Jacques Rebibo, Alex Ferranti, Neale Donald Walsch, Don Miguel Ruiz, Julie Bondanza, Renee Monroe, Rick Dutra-St. John, Yvonne St. John-Dutra, Rebecca Huss-Ashmore, Lynn Twist, Cynthia Smith Austin, Angelo D'Amelio, Carol O'Hara, Laurel Scheaf, Brian Regnier, Marilou Bova, Sondra Ray, Julia Dederer, Kalindi, Eugenie Starr, and Jodi Gold.

There have been many more and I apologize for not naming you specifically, but please know I hold you in my heart.

I wish to acknowledge my friends who have contributed to the writing of this book. Each of you has had a unique influence in making this a better book. It truly has been a team effort.

Most of you will know what it was you said or did, but a few of you might wonder. I know, and it made a difference, and I profoundly thank each and every one of you.

Alan Mesher, Ann Contois, Beverly Goldman, Bill Arrott, Bill Marjenhoff, Bob Luckin, Boca Raton Writing Group, Carolyn Baker, Cynthia Cavalcanti, Dale Ledbetter, David Presler, Don Pet, Elaine Colton, Elizabeth Arrott, Gail Gulino, George Sasdi, Jim Selman, Jon Mackler, Judith Churchman, Lois Bender, Lulu Farrell, Margaret Stortz, Mark Levine, Maryann Karinch, Michael Vita, Miksha Garg, Niki Faldemolaei, Philip Elton Collins, Ray Lekowski, Rechee Huff, Rob Sigal, Rod Schwarz, Ron Pevny, Sam Daley-Harris, Sandy Belsley, Shelli Blair, Steven Smith. Tim Farrell, Virginia Aronson, Martin Cohen, Maurice Cohen, Valerie Porter, and Mary VanMeer.

Preface: The Quiet Desperation

Glenda had volunteered to read an early draft of *Elders Rock!*

"Oh Harvey, you have tapped into something so deep and so powerful." Pause. "And so unspoken."

"You wrote that older people sometimes 'live lives of quiet desperation.' I wonder if you really know how bad it can be for women."

"Tell me," I replied.

Sadness crept into her voice.

"I remember it so well. I was at the heart of my family, loved, happy and living life to the fullest. Yet at the same time, there was something else there, some unspoken and unnamed yearning. Only now can I look back and name it a little. And it wasn't just me. I have spoken with so many other women of this. I'll just say it for me but it's not about just me. It is about so many of us.

"I felt foggy. I felt like I was quietly grasping for something out of my reach. There was an elusive quality, like I wasn't really in control. There was a sense of having lost my way.

"People told me how great my life was, and they were right, really right. Yet, there was a kind of 'just putting one foot in front of the other' quality to it. It was like my role had disappeared and I was drifting. A kind of 'why bother' because nothing really matters.

"I had the sense I was trying to control something I couldn't control and didn't know why I couldn't. But felt I ought to be able to. There was a loose-ends quality to it. Like something was over and nothing had started … because it couldn't."

I found myself weeping as she spoke. Yes, I did know. Perhaps not to the depth she spoke of it for women, but I knew it for myself and for so many men. I believe it is the source of the phony camaraderie of men, that chatter at the water cooler and in the locker room.

It underlies the emphasis on watching professional sports … old men watching strong young men … and "Hey, how about them Redskins!" I, too, knew this loss of direction, this wondering "what's next" and being afraid my future might be nothing but more of the same.

This was why I brought one life to a close and started my life all over again.

Yes, *lives of quiet desperation.* How beautifully that expresses it. And as Thoreau, who first wrote it, adds, *"... and dying with their song unsung."* I was unable to write this without wailing, leaning backward so the tears will not land on my computer keyboard.

"How in hell," I wondered, "did I get born into this time, this pretentious glitch! Why was I born into this time when we have so lost our way as human beings, born into this time of feeling separate and lonely, yet unable to articulate what's wrong?"

This is why I wrote this book. It is for all of us men and for all of us women who have that deep sense that there is a "terrible missing." Perhaps the route back to our purposeful humanity is via Elder and what Elder has always meant deep in our ancient "heart of hearts."

Perhaps, just perhaps....

Introduction

This book is unique and it is powerful. Its main purpose is to coach you to become a wise Elder. We all age but most people just get older, not wiser. This book is for those who suspect there is much more to life than merely aging.

Elderhood is our vanished Third Stage of Life, a marvelous stage, for which the first two stages – Youth and Adult – are supposed to prepare us. At one time they did. Now they don't. In this age of technology, Elderhood has been sidelined, ignored, and disempowered.

I am an Elder. I love my life. I have written this book because I am committed to restoring our distinctive stage of Elderhood – wise, compassionate, and cherished.

This book is my invitation for you to join me on this journey. As you use this book to coach yourself, you will gain wisdom, freedom, and enormous satisfaction. To be a wise and contributing Elder is to live a life you love. Your family will be better for it and you will leave a more powerful legacy.

And the world will be a better place because you have lived.

* * * * *

Elders Rock! is divided into two books.

Book One is the story of how we lost our natural and critical Third Stage of Life, Elderhood.

Book Two is a guide to becoming a wise Elder and supporting others on this path. While the second book can stand alone, its value rests on understanding the story of what happened to our Third Stage of Life.

Together, there are Ten Themes:

1. For eons, Elderhood stood powerfully as our natural Third Stage of Life. We have lost the Wisdom of Elder.

2. Elderhood is the stage of wisdom, compassion, and joy – life in full bloom. Elders have gained a profound understanding of the world-as-it-is. They are the reservoir of both the secular and the spiritual history of our species, and they use their knowledge for the good of all. Their longer view allows Elders to see the patterns of life clearly and to look down the path for many generations.

Elders are attuned with the Earth and with Spirit. Elders live in the Now with an open heart, and they have the capacity both to smile at the follies of the past and to create new possibilities for the future. They serve as models for the young.

Elders are unafraid, and they live in the quietness of the lessened vigor of their bodies. They no longer focus on the avoidance of pain or the obsession with comfort. Elders laugh easily and tread lightly on the earth.

3. A three-stage life – Youth, Adult and Elder – is virtually unique to human beings. All other species

have only a two-stage life – Youth and Adult – the female dying when she can no longer produce young.

4. The human female is unique because she does not die. She, no longer a *pro*-creator, has another 30 to 40 years to live, a half-lifetime or more. Perhaps evolution's unique role for post-reproductive woman is that of Wise Woman, *co*-creator of humanity's greatness.

5. We began to lose Elderhood about 5000 years ago with the formation of towns and cities. This loss of Elder intensified 200 years ago with the discovery of the colossal energy from fossil fuels. Along with the loss of Elder, we have developed a swollen stage of Adulthood, insatiable in its quest for more and more without regard for planetary consequences.

6. We have lost family, the natural training ground for Elder. Nothing has replaced it.

7. The future for humanity rests solidly on its worldview. During this period, our global worldview has shifted from the eons-long You AND Me worldview of inclusion and cooperation, to our present adversarial worldview of You OR Me. This competitive worldview is both unstable and unsustainable. This global shift of worldview is both an evolutionary back-step and a threat to the very existence of humankind.

8. Restoration of the Third Stage of Life – Elder with its wisdom – is crucial to regaining the natural balance of human life on our planet.

9. The attributes of Elder live in the realm of Being. They are distinct from and transcend the *doing-ness* traits of Adult.

10. Elder-Training best occurs in groups and consists of powerful conversations and exercises to emphasize Elder attributes – creativity, vulnerability, integrity, responsibility and communication.

The exercises and distinctions in this book create a powerful path to the Wisdom of Elder and can create a magnificent future for you, for those you love, and for humanity.

I am committed to your journey and I hope you will find my words valuable to your life. It is critical that you remain open to possibility and to new ideas. In the pages that follow, there are many of both.

Keep what is of value to you. Discard what is not.

Book One is a story about how the world got to be the way it is. It is not a story about who, what, when and where. Nor is it about which nations conquered others. Rather it is a story painted with the broadest of strokes. It is the most basic story of all, a story of shifting worldviews.

No history can ever be a true story, implying that this is *really* the way it happened, because all stories are told through a filter. All are subjective and have both a point of view and a purpose. The history of a war, for instance, is usually told from the point of view of the winner. One told by the loser would be strikingly different.

This story's point of view stands outside the confines of most histories.

This place of observation allows you to examine two human worldviews. The first of these, the You AND Me worldview, generates and supports the Elder stage of life. The second, our present worldview, You OR Me, does not.

My intention is for this book to support your co-creation, with others, of the evolving worldview of You AND Me, wherein all life is celebrated and no one is left out.

In Book Two, I present the technology of training yourself to become an Elder. This is the heart of the book. This know-how is based on my own forty years of knowledge and experience with self-training models that work.

The ultimate goal is to restore Elderhood to its natural and respected position as the Third Stage of Life – wise, compassionate, and cherished. This, I believe, is critical for humanity's upward evolution.

* * * * *

I have chosen to use feminine gender pronouns in this book: she, her, and hers. This may seem awkward for the male reader. I ask you to please be willing to adjust. Woman is culturally evolving to take her rightful powerful role in our world and I wish to honor and underscore her importance.

BOOK ONE
ELDERHOOD

My Story

"Gentlemen, you have a serious problem."

Dean Wiggers stared down at us from behind his podium. We were first-year medical students, most of us twenty-two years old, sitting up straight in our best jackets, white shirts, and ties. It was a warm September day in Albany, New York. The year was 1957 and it was our first day in medical school. We looked at each other in consternation. Was the school closing down?

"The problem is this. Fifty percent of what we shall teach you here will be wrong." The dean paused. "Unfortunately, we do not know which fifty percent that is." He smiled at us gently. "Gentlemen, have an interesting life." Then the dean sat down.

My classmates looked upset. I wasn't. I was energized. This was because I knew in my heart he had spoken the truth. For me his small speech was a grand epiphany. I was finally where I belonged – in a place where I would hear *truths.*

The Early Story

I was born in a time and place where education was limited. I grew up in a small town in the jewelry industry of southeast New England. Mom was a factory worker, Pop a postal clerk. We were not a close-knit family, although Sundays were spent with relatives. We had the trappings of normalcy within the New England way of behaving … reserved, rarely hugging, and never speaking from the heart.

Deep in my own heart, which felt like a rock in my chest, lay the belief I had somehow been born at the wrong time and in the wrong place. I also had the sense there was something wrong around me. I suspected I was being constantly lied to – by everybody.

Oh, they were nice enough, particularly the folks on my paper route. But it felt to me like adults never told us kids what was really going on. Yet my parents told me always to obey adults. Face to face, adults were nice to each other; out of sight, they weren't. I was confused.

I knew I would not stay in that tiny town with its population of 2000 and a high school graduating class of fourteen. Most people did, but I could not. I pushed my curiosity and innate intelligence, working and studying hard so that I might get away as fast as I could.

I always found time to read. I read everything I could find, hoping to discover some truths about life. My parents' home had a bookcase containing only monthly copies of *Reader's Digest* and a tattered encyclopedia set from 1897 that my grandfather had given my father. After my parents saved up to buy me a new *Encyclopedia Americana* set for my sixteenth birthday, I read practically every word in every volume.

This gift of kindness, so far above my parents' means, was one of the most important presents I ever received, one that spurred my thirst for knowledge. "Look it up!" my father would reply whenever I asked a question. With that encyclopedia set, I could do so. And I did.

Though money was scarce, my parents were supportive of my life plans. We all knew college would be my way out. When I was old enough, I chose a state university in Amherst, ninety miles away. This seemed to me like the other side of the world.

One of my hometown heroes was our local doctor, Hyman Lillien, M.D. Dr. Lillien had birthed me, cared for my well-being, and at times mentored me. He inspired me to pursue a career in medicine. After four years of undergraduate school, I applied to medical school. By that time I was married. We moved to a single room on the second floor of Mitchell Koldy's Photography Studio for my last few months of college.

The idea of becoming a doctor felt both remote and terrifying. I surprised myself and most who knew me when I was accepted to Albany Medical College. With the holes in the soles of my shoes lined with cardboard, I moved with my new wife to a tiny apartment in the poorest section of Albany. We drove there in our eleven-year-old car that rarely started without a push.

Then, on the first day of medical school, I finally heard it. A TRUTH. Yes! It seemed like the first truth I had ever heard.

The Pretense That We Know

Dean Wiggers' words caused a shift in my life. His words had acknowledged and underscored my intuition that I had been living in a culture of make-believe, a culture that was somehow *wrong*. He had, with his amazing and unexpected remark, exposed the underbelly of a monstrous pretense … the pretense that *we really know*.

I suddenly was able to label the lie I had been born into and had been living inside of my whole life – a massive pretense that *we already had all the answers*. It was instantly clear to me why I had felt constantly lied to. I had been.

My Secret: Fear

During those years, my greatest fear was that everyone would find out I was only a frightened little boy from New England, and they would push me to the side. Even though I had run a small business – I had an ice cream truck for four years to fund college, I was inexperienced in the world outside my small town.

I had a dark grey lump in the center of my chest, a lump of fear that was constantly present.

At the same time, I was certain there was more to life. I don't mean the usual trappings that arrive with success. No, I felt that I had some greater purpose, one yet unknown and unfulfilled.

I seldom spoke up during college and medical school. After all, I had to keep my fear hidden. However, I knew how to ask certain kinds of questions to open up areas our classroom discussions overlooked. One time I was told by a teacher, "You have a great talent." I was thrilled to hear this. Then he added, "… for pointing out the obvious."

I was embarrassed and believed I'd overstepped some secret boundary and became even more quiet. It took years before I realized this was indeed a talent. I discovered that some things became obvious only *after* I had pointed them out.

My quest for truth resulted in success. I completed the four years of medical school, graduating with an M.D. degree. After three additional years of general surgical training and two more years of training in plastic surgery, I passed the oral and written examinations and became Board Certified in Plastic and Reconstructive Surgery.

Successful Career

I settled in Pittsburgh, opened a solo practice, and was appointed to the staff of five hospitals. Soon I was busy enough to take on a junior partner. This was a big deal for me, for the frightened little boy from Plainville. I felt like the protagonist in the Horatio Alger story – small town boy makes good in the big city.

By that time, I had a family, a lovely home, a vacation farm, and a sports car. I had worked hard my entire life to get to this point, doing anything and everything to become who I was. I had delivered newspapers, tied fishing flies, washed windows, and swept the floor of a machine shop, as well as working seventy hours a week for four summers as Harvey the Ice Cream Man, selling Popsicles, Fudgicles, and Push-ups.

Finally, *I had arrived.*

Yet, the lump in my chest was still there. In fact, the fear was deeper and heavier than ever. It was still my deepest secret.

They say still waters run deep. They don't. Still waters run putrid.

Crack in the Cosmic Egg

In my early years as a surgeon, if you had asked me what I was looking for, I would not have been able to tell you. I simply knew the following: who and what I was being wasn't it.

The Crack in the Cosmic Egg by Joseph Chilton Pearce was written more than forty years ago. He speaks of the cosmic egg as the set of cultural agreements, rules and standards we all live inside of, like a great egg. A crack in the shell occurs at the moment of an epiphany, where one abruptly discovers there is something *off* with the culture. The title is a good metaphor for the epiphany I had when Dean Wiggers "cracked the egg" for me. At that moment, it became clear that I had lived my life inside the "cosmic egg of agreed-upon pretense."

I held on to that epiphany. I held on long enough to make it more real. In fact, I adopted this slogan to help with spotting truths: "Distinguish the mushroom from the horse manure it grows in. They are both brown, but only one is edible."

Twenty Years Later, the Midlife Crisis

There are paradoxes that can paralyze a person and I was in the middle of one.

On the one hand, I was living the American dream and was quite used to it. Periodically I would tell the worn-out story of Dean Wiggers' insightful words. Success was easy to get used to. I had a large home, a Porsche, a wonderful practice, a vacation farm and children. My cosmic egg had re-intacted, all the cracks filled in as smooth as alabaster.

On the other hand, this life that looked so right from the outside felt so wrong on the inside. I felt as off-kilter when I was approaching my fortieth birthday as I had when I was a kid in that town.

I was angry and I didn't know why. I worked long hours at my practice but I was vaguely dissatisfied with my work. When I was home, I was vaguely dissatisfied with my home life. I felt victimized by my upbringing, and I blamed everyone. I vaguely resented the life I had chosen. I was a walking contradiction – I was successful yet I was pissed off about it.

Whenever I couldn't sleep I stayed up reading magazines. One sleepless night, I stumbled upon an article in *Cosmopolitan.* Marcia Seligson had written an exposé of a new four-day training program in California called ***est***.

The article was conflicted because the author had received so much value from the training she was unable to write an exposé. Instead, she admitted that after the program, she had reclaimed her relationship with her mother, stopped taking sleeping pills, and broken off a detrimental relationship.

Her vulnerability and truthfulness struck me at a deep level. I recognized she had spoken from her heart. I was both touched and moved to action. Yet, my normal cynicism was still present. I thought maybe her heartfelt-ness was not real.

The *est* Training

The next morning, I felt both desperate and hopeful. I called the nearest *est* venue, which was five hours away in Washington, D.C., and registered for the two-weekend course. (The course has since evolved into a three-day educational experience known as The Landmark Forum, an initial course of their three-part Curriculum for Living.)

I attended, but I was skeptical. With all of my medical training, I was certain I would discover the lie, the hypocrisy. Instead, my life transformed. During those four days, I discovered how much my education, those thirteen years of formal education beyond high school, had missed the truth.

I had two major realizations during that amazing

pair of weekends. First, I discovered that I have an automatic inner voice that never stops talking. I had simply assumed that the voice was *me.* Instead I discovered the little voice was something I *had* rather than something I *was.* Moreover, I discovered that everyone else had one too.

The trainer referred to the voice as "the mind talking." We will explore this concept in depth later in the book.

The Fear Disappeared

The second revelation of the two weekends at *est* was even more major. The lump in my chest disappeared. During a single hour-long process, my fear reduced significantly. In fact, on a scale of 100, my fear level fell from a 95 to 5! Fear had been *the* secret of my life. Fear *was* the lump in my chest.

What happened for me in the process was so simple it sounds absurd. *I discovered everyone has fear.* As bizarre as this may seem, I simply had not known that. Rather, I was certain I was the *only* fearful one.

Over time, I had become a closed book, withdrawn and careful, never revealing myself. I had hidden behind the professional mask of the surgeon. This kept me from knowing anyone else. After all, my mind insisted, if I got to know *you,* then you would get to know *me.* I could not let that happen. I have since discovered this sense of not belonging is known as shame. And shame is virtually universal.

No wonder my marriage was going down the drain. I didn't know who she was and I hadn't let her know her who I was, or how afraid I was. And I had been afraid of everything, including commitment, marriage, and children.

The moment I discovered everyone else had fear, I felt admitted to the human race. And I was face to face with the realization that it was my own fear that had kept me out.

I was deeply shaken.

My Ladder of Success Was Leaning on the Wrong Wall

> *"Culture ... a collection of learned survival strategies passed on to our young through teaching and modeling."* – Joseph Chilton Pearce

At *est,* I saw that I had climbed the ladder of success, only to discover *my ladder had been leaning against the wrong wall.* The wall I had chosen was built of the loose bricks sanctioned by our culture – competitiveness, grades, degrees, published papers, and prizes, as well as a fine family, a big house, a new automobile, and an enviable income.

Even though I had the agreement of the world that I was a small town boy who had made it, deep down I knew I had sold out. I wasn't doing what I had been born to do. I didn't yet know what that was.

But now I knew that what my culture said was the *right* life and the *best* life was not for me.

In the face of that profound realization, I cried for a month. These were strange tears. I would get into my car each morning and cry all the way to my first hospital. I would dry my tears, make rounds on my patients, climb back into the car, and cry my way to the next hospital.

I was not depressed. I had entered into the profound grief of having lived for forty years in fear and disconnection from others. And I realized I could not blame others, because I was the one responsible for my life. And now I could envision how different, how transformed, my life could be. What a relief!

I also understood that my new realization by itself would not be enough to make a difference in my life. I needed to take some definitive action so the second half of my life would not become an automatic extension of the first half.

I Bring My Life to a Close

> *"To change one's life, start immediately, do it flamboyantly, no exceptions."* – William James

> *"Your time is limited, so don't waste it living someone else's life. Don't let the noise of others' opinions drown out your inner voice."* – Steve Jobs

It took a year, and there were times when I trembled with fear, but I brought my life as I had known it to a close. I was determined I would begin my life again from a clear place, as open and vulnerable as a child, regardless of how much time I had wasted.

I am not advocating that you leave your work, your family, or your home. I am simply stating there is far more to life than most of us suspect. I chose to act on that understanding. I had found my path.

I sold my practice to my partner. I took my entire net worth (about $300,000 in 1976 dollars) and paid off the mortgage on my house. I also set up funds to provide for my family's expenses and education for my children.

Then I left it all behind – my practice, my profession, my family, the city I called home, the money I had saved, and all my possessions.

I left behind everything I had mistakenly identified with and I went out into the world to find out who I really was.

Life in a Pickup Truck

This may sound like a classic midlife crisis. Who knows? I leaped in fully. I left the American dream behind. By leaving that life, so widely honored but so conventional, I was able to discover how much more to life there really is.

I embarked on a two-year journey as a vagabond, living in a camper on the back of a pickup truck. I owned virtually nothing, and spent my time traveling up and down the East Coast. The truck was old and my mattress extended above the cab. I slept every night on its softness under a brown alpaca throw. I reveled in being alone.

Sometimes I turned the wheel to the right, traveling first here, then turning left there, for the where-ness mattered little. I met strangers everywhere and talked with new people in new places. I was vulnerable and spoke freely of my hopes and dreams. I wanted nothing to keep me separate from people ever again. I was a person among persons.

I kept one secret, though. Remembering how awkward conversations sometimes became when I said I was a surgeon, I kept one secret … that I had been a doctor. I doubted anyone would believe me anyway, and some things are better left unspoken.

I remember a day when, parked at a Days Inn campground in Orlando, Florida, I met a portly fellow there who was persistent. "What do you do for a living?"

"I'm unemployed."

"OK, but what did you do before?"

"Well, I was a … well … yeah … I was *a plastic surgeon.*"

Clearly not believing, he changed the subject. I was delighted because it's not easy to make the truth sound like a lie. Once a serious surgeon living a serious life, I was beginning to find amusement in small things.

I learned the quiet pleasure of hanging out with people, and that a canoe trip down a wilderness stream with a clear view to a sandy bottom six feet below, can be a source of awe. I was brought to tears by a flock of pelicans flying in formation in and out of a fog bank at dawn.

I experienced the profound loneliness of having no one to speak with for several days in a row. I really got that these moments represented my life in its fullness, a life which was occurring *now,* not as some pale dress rehearsal for a life *someday.*

I laughed a lot. I walked around sometimes with my mouth hanging open in amazement. And sometimes I wept, quietly in joy, or loudly in grief. In short, I felt so alive, so fully human.

A True Vacating

Walking out of my life was painful to those who depended on me.

However, my choice was one of the wisest life shifts I ever made, and certainly the one requiring the most courage. I was on a vacation in the truest sense of the word. After all, to take a vacation means to vacate.

I had vacated my life as I had known it so that I could stand outside it, review it, and create my life anew. I had needed to examine myself without the encumbrances of obligation, prior choices, or the culture I had lived within.

It was not an easy period in my life, but one that was very worthwhile.

I now had a clearing, an open space in which to create a vision for my future. I knew, given time and freedom, I would create a future to pull me into something new and engaging. It was a completely new way of being. And I loved it.

My Bright New World

Twenty-two months later, I completed my journey. Aborigines call such a journey a *walk-about,* while others refer to it as a vision quest. I had named mine a "Chautauqua" (pronounced *shuh-tok'wa*) after a historical cultural trail in New York State and Canada.

I entered a bright new world – a world where I vowed I would never again do anything I did not freely choose to do. I entered a world where I was a beginner, a world where possibility reigned, a world where all could be questioned.

I declared that my life was my life and *I* was fully in charge of it. All assumptions and rules and ideas were up for examination.

At age forty, my life had begun again at an exciting new level. I was beginning to see people newly, less through the lenses of fear and distrust, and I found them both interesting and good. I developed a new depth of empathy for people. They now occurred as warmer, somehow. And I was freer to be me – fun, exciting and really okay.

I Return to Medicine

Prior to my Chautauqua, I had been the senior partner of a Plastic and Reconstructive Surgery Practice in Pittsburgh. Our practice had spanned the entire spectrum of the specialty … trauma of the face and hand, the treatment of burns, and surgery for cancer of the head and neck.

But what I had loved doing most was cosmetic surgery. This kind of plastic surgery just felt right to me. It was comfortable, as though cosmetic surgery and I were a match.

This turned out to be accurate. Unlike the reputation cosmetic surgery had in some circles, creating superficial changes for superficial people, my experience of the practice was different. I saw cosmetic surgery as something that served a greater purpose.

I was not interested in the vain and foolish. Rather, I wanted to bring to life the hidden dreams each of us have, dreams masked by time, injury, and genetics. So I re-entered medicine, daring to be the first plastic surgeon in the country to arrive at a new city and announce a practice of *exclusively* cosmetic surgery.

I chose to live in Washington, D.C., because I had done the *est* training there, and I considered the city my spiritual home. I founded my cosmetic surgery practice in the lovely suburb of McLean, Virginia.

Cosmetic surgery was still a rarity in 1978, especially in that conservative city of suits and politicians; and launching my practice was an uphill climb. During those first years, I barely made expenses. Sometimes I used one credit card to pay off another.

Later, after I had re-established myself, my children left Pittsburgh one by one. As young adults, they chose to live close.

Eating, Breathing and Sleeping Cosmetic Surgery

I loved cosmetic surgery. For me, the purpose of cosmetic surgery was to relieve the suffering of those whose appearance was off, inconsistent with society's demanding and absurd standards for beauty and youth.

I could empathize with the suffering of those who had been sidelined by our culture, viewed as *less-than* because they didn't match the standards. I saw the pain of beautiful women who had become invisible as they aged, their wrinkles of experience not a testament but a detriment.

Our culture ignores both the plain and the old. Yet, every one of us remains beautiful and youthful on the inside. In my hands, my patients' outer appearance could be enhanced or altered to more closely match their inner self.

Practicing this art provided me with the marvelous opportunity to observe the inner transformation that can follow an outer transformation.

Together we, patient and doctor as a team, could uplift a downturned mouth to match inner happiness. Or remove the family frown and hear afterwards that "people are greeting me again. I have become visible." Their suffering was individual but the source was our culture with its bizarre standards of appearance.

It was good and it was so satisfying to work with these courageous patients. As Ellen, first a patient and now my wife of nearly twenty years, says, "Now, when I look in the mirror, it looks like me – the way I pictured myself, the way I was supposed to look. I don't rush by mirrors any more. I am willing to go without makeup, even in my late sixties. It was such a blessing for me to feel whole again."

The Ontologic Laboratory

In a sense, my practice became an ontological laboratory. Ontology is the study of the "being" of human beings. Ontology differs from psychology in that psychology studies the *differences* between us, while ontology is the study of the *sameness* of every one of us – the core of commonality that makes us each a human being.

I was profoundly impressed by how much a patient's personality shifted when they trusted me to alter their misleading outer mask. These alterations not only revealed their natural inner self, but they began to radiate confidence and enthusiasm. They walked with a new step. They became more *real.* They fell in love with themselves, and they fell in love with life.

The Core Questions

I felt privileged to participate in the journey of expansion they experienced. I found myself living inside of these core questions: "What is the being of human beings?" and "What role does physicality play in transformation?"

Before we began, I asked my patients to reveal themselves with questions like: "Why did you really come to see me?" and "How do you expect cosmetic surgery to impact your life?"

Post-operatively, I asked them: "Now, what can you teach me, as your partner in this journey, about what cosmetic surgery is *really* for?" and "Did you *actually* become younger after your surgery or was it simply that you *look* younger?"

I even asked them: "If you feel you have become younger, do you believe you will now *live longer?*" A study at the Mayo Clinic had suggested that this may indeed be the case.

Renewal of the Search for Truth

I re-invented myself as a searcher of truth. And, in serving my patients, I had learned the lessons of kindness, compassion, and how to listen with an open heart.

My practice thrived. My partners and our staff supported me as I published medical articles and book chapters and gave lectures to audiences of plastic surgeons worldwide – Belgium, Mexico, Sweden, and Brazil.

The practice I founded still thrives as The Austin-Weston Center for Cosmetic Surgery in Reston, Virginia. It has become one of the largest free-standing cosmetic surgery practices in the United States, with four Board-Certified Plastic Surgeons and a staff of thirty-five.

In 2003, after forty-six years in the field of medicine, I retired from my surgical practice. I was sixty-eight and about to begin the third act of the play called *My Life*.

My Parallel Story

Here I must back up. Over the course of almost forty years, I attended more than fifty courses. Some lasted a single day, others took place over a weekend. I also attended several ten-day residential courses and two years of learning within in a California-based Mystery School. *(A semi-chronological list of my coursework is included in Appendix 2.)* Intuition determined which course I took, and in what order.

Life's Big Questions

I took most of the courses during the years of my surgical practice. These trainings, retreats, and workshops represented thousands of hours of exposure to master teachers of self-discovery, inquiry, and reorientation. These courses, in addition to what my patients taught me, became my own personal wisdom training.

In retrospect, this was my work as an Elder-in-training.

In the courses I took, we looked at some of the biggest questions of Life:

Who am I?

Why am I here?

What is life all about?

What is *my* life all about?

Over time, I got clear about my answers:

I am a spiritual being having a human experience.

I am here to know my talents and gifts and apply them in world service.

I am here to learn to love all things and life itself.

I am here to fully experience this thrilling world of space-time boundaries.

The Third Act

Upon retiring from my surgical practice, my astute wife moved me away from the rapid-paced Washington D.C. area to the calmer Eastern Shore of Maryland. She sensed I would not easily make the shift from surgeon to the next phase of life. She believed I would have hung out at the practice, annoyed the other surgeons and, most importantly, betrayed myself.

It became clear to me that moving away from my practice was a physical manifestation reflecting my inner shift. And although I hated to admit it, my wife was right.

The Waiting Place

I found myself in Dr. Seuss's "Waiting Place" (*Oh, the Places You'll Go!*). For a half dozen years, I was living my life, even loving my life, and watching my retirement play out.

It was not so much that *I* waited. It seemed more like the *waiting waited me.*

During this time, I gave up the silent but tenacious god – ISA; that is, an addiction to Importance, Significance, and Achievement. Instead, I took on the worship of an odd new god, George Q. Puttering. I became a devotee of high level puttering. I sculpted, I wrote, I workshopped. I made the bed and I walked the dog.

I puttered.

The Quest for Truth Resurges

The time in that waiting place left me in a calm place, an open place. Then the search for TRUTH insisted its way back into my life.

I am aware *truth* has too many caps, for one can never know *the* truth. Any attempt on my part to convince you of anything being *the* truth would be arrogant.

All I can do is use metaphor and story to point at what I have found especially useful. And I do love pointing to the lessons I have learned.

Over the years, in addition to being a searcher, I had also become a writer, a speaker, and a teacher.

World Citizen – To Be in World Service

My questions had widened beyond my own personal growth. I had long viewed myself as a world citizen, so my questions began to reflect an expanded view of myself-as-humanity.

In 1991, I went to Senegal with The Hunger Project, an organization committed to ending hunger in the world. I found the Senegalese to be just like me, differing only in that they were poorer in goods but richer in spirit.

I found similar results during Hunger Project trips to India, Burkina Faso, and Bangladesh. The villagers were looking for opportunities to make a difference in their lives. But, unlike me, a typical person of the so-called first world, they did not hunger for connection with Spirit. Of Spirit they had an abundance.

I have had the opportunity to see firsthand some of the forty percent of the world, our brothers and sisters, who live on less than four dollars per day. We in the first world have a strange attitude. To use a baseball metaphor, we were lucky enough to be born on third base, yet we act as if we had hit a triple.

My questions, originally so personal, became much bigger: What are the trends occurring in the world? Where is evolution taking humans? What is humanity's role in co-evolving ourselves?

Student of Humanity's Future

As a global citizen I developed a broad outlook. I became a student of possible futures for our world and I have done my homework. I've read thousands of pages of reports and articles from governmental agencies and think tanks, scores of interpretive articles by futurists, scientists, and wise visionaries. I've spent many hours listening to interviews, watching TED talks and YouTube videos.

My reading, phone conversations, e-mails, and group discussions all had the underlying purpose of discovering where our human species is headed and what corrections we must make to ensure a better future.

The Trimtab

Before we enter into our exploration of Elderhood, I wish to tell you about an incident that had a powerful effect upon me.

In 1977, while on the logistics team for an event held at Constitution Hall in Washington, D.C., I had the pleasure of meeting Buckminster Fuller. Werner Erhard, the founder of *est,* introduced Dr. Fuller to a packed house. Then the two men spoke to each other and to the audience. For seven hours.

I was struck by what Bucky said. These words have become a cornerstone of my life. In fact, this book has arisen from them. Paraphrased:

> If you wish to alter the direction of the Great Ship of State, don't just jump off the ship and try to push the bow around. Go instead to the rear where the rudder is.

> You are too small to move the rudder, but on the back of the rudder is a smaller rudder called the trimtab. To move it, take its wheel and turn it and turn it for a long time. This moves the trimtab which moves the rudder which alters the direction of the great Ship of State.
>
> To locate the trimtab, discover what is wanted and needed. And produce it.

The YouTube video is located at:

https://www.youtube.com/watch?v=KxS0dSZPz9A. The "trimtab" section is at 42:14. (You can also search, "Werner Erhard Interviews Buckminster Fuller.")

You and I are at the rudder of our great ship, *Humanity's Future.* Might you be searching for the trimtab as I have? Might you also be asking, "What is wanted and needed?"

Can you hold the possibility that Elder, or perhaps you as Elder, might be precisely what is wanted and needed? And that *the restoration of Elderhood as our natural Third Stage of Life* might be the trimtab that will turn the Great Ship of Humanity?

We can't really "get" life until we have lived long enough and had enough experiences to have a broad perspective. Elders have gone through the good and the bad and the ups and the downs enough so that, finally, wisdom is possible.

Unfortunately the Great Ship no longer honors Elder, yet Elder not only serves as the sacred guardian of the trimtab, but might be the trimtab itself.

Let's now begin our exploration of Elder as humanity's natural Third Stage of Life.

Stages of Life

To understand the term Elder, let's look at Elder and Elderhood from the perspective of a natural hierarchy of life.

Natural Hierarchy of Life

There are many ways one can assess a lifetime. The division of a lifetime into stages is arbitrary and designed to support a particular focus. The focus of this book is twofold: upon your becoming an Elder, and upon the possibility of re-establishing the powerful role of Elder worldwide.

I have divided the natural hierarchy of life in the traditional manner, that is, into three stages: Youth, Adult, and Elder. I further distinguish Youth as having two segments – Child and Pre-Adult (adolescent).

ELDER

ADULT

YOUTH: Child, Pre-Adult

I have not included "the aged" as a stage because they are not our focus. For the purpose of this book, we shall consider "the aged" as being those old people who are no longer able to care for themselves as a result of physical and/or mental infirmity. William H. Thomas, M.D., author of the books, *What Are Old People For?* and *Second Wind,* considers the aged to be a special case in our society. He believes they make a major contribution to community life. This book is not about that group (see Appendix 1).

There is nothing inherently right or wrong in distinguishing stages of life this way. You can think of this model as *useful,* rather than definitive or correct.

Stages of Life, Not Ages of Life

It is important to realize these are *stages* of life and not *ages* of life. Nonetheless, we might, just as a generality, speak of Youth as being from age 0-25, Adult as being from 25-60, and Elder as 60 on.

However, stages only roughly correlate with ages. There are fifty-year-olds who are not yet Adults and twenty-year-olds who are indeed Adult. Moreover, there are many people over sixty who have not entered the stage of Elder, and might never do so. There are also a few adults, some in their twenties, who seem so wise, kind, compassionate, and other-centered that they deserve to be considered Elders.

Tribe as Model

We have a present-day model for these stages in the worldwide indigenous tribes with their natural way of living over thousands of years. There are 240 tribes of indigenous people in Brazil alone, according to http://SurvivalInternational.org.

So I will speak of tribe both as a *reality* of countless indigenous tribes and as a *metaphor for small human communities.* Also, for ease of speaking, I will speak of tribe and village interchangeably.

Role of Child

In the village (metaphorically and literally), the role of Child is to be young, full of joy and enthusiasm, imbued with a sense of oneness with everything. The world is theirs to explore, everything to be related to and everyone to love and be loved by.

Child's schoolyard is the woods, the fields, the ponds, the birds, the animals. Also the shops, the neighboring homes, the whole village. Those in the stage of Child learn the ways of their parents and grandparents and the extended family – the entire village. They also begin to live in relationship with their far-extended family, the rest of the living world.

Child lives in the realm of the joy of BEING.

Role of Pre-Adult (adolescent)

The purpose of the Pre-Adult is to learn the ways of their culture – how to relate to others in ways that work. They discover what work they love, are attracted to and adapted for. They learn the means of more formal communication.

In the Western world we call this the basics, our symbolic language of reading, writing, and arithmetic. It is also the time of learning the remainder of whatever information may underpin the particular culture. Pre-Adult apprentices itself to the ways of Adult, learning how to function in the world. It is also the time of sexual exploration.

Pre-Adult learns to adjust individual desires so as to integrate them with the dictates of their culture, often in opposition. The individual instinctively wants to do *what* she wants, *when* she wants and *how* she wants.

The culture, by contrast, maintains itself by regimenting each individual into the role of contributing member. Therefore, Pre-Adult has the task of learning how to dance with these two opposing forces.

Of critical importance is the task of staying open to new thinking. Ideally, those in Pre-Adult select their own teachers. The mind that stays curious, receptive, and discerning is both learnable and teachable.

Pre-Adult lives in the realm of the joy of Being and DOING.

Role of Adult

Adult is the fully-developed, in-the-world human. It is the time of procreation and co-creation of the new family unit. It is the time of raising children and passing on knowledge and interpretation of the world. It is the time for exploration of the fullness and expression of aptitudes and goals.

It is a time of self-expansion as individual, the time of expansion of self-as-relationship, and the time of expansion of self-as-group, primarily as expressed in family. It becomes the time to produce results in-the-world. It is the time of citizenry.

Adult lives in the realm of the joy of DOING. In the middle and later years of Adult, as one approaches the Elder stage, there is a shift into the joy of both DOING and Being.

Role of Elder

Elder is the culmination. It is the time when everything comes together. Elder is the full expression of knowing who one is in one's entirety, not just as individual, but also self-as-relationship, self-as-group, and self-as-Spirit.

One sees the larger picture of life, first dimly, then with leaps of increasing clarity. We shall examine Elder with great intensity later in the book.

Elder is a time of joy of BEING. The role of BEING expands to include Doing – doing whatever there is to be done. It is the time of full Self-Expression.

It is the time of the greatest joy of both BEING and Doing.

Conversations at Each Stage

YOUTH

Child: “Little Harvey is just so active!”

Pre-Adult: “Harv is a quick learner and gets the job done.”

ADULT: “Mr. Harvey is a great leader.”

ELDER: “Let us ask Baba Harvey. He will listen and advise us from his wisdom.”

When one is complete and considered “aged,” others might ask: “Whose day is it to have the privilege of bringing Baba Harvey his food and taking him out for a ride?”

Now let’s look what it means for us to just … get … older. And, later, contrast it strongly with what it means to become an *Elder* – wise, compassionate and cherished.

Language Matters

> *"ALL THINGS ARE POSSIBLE to him who believes in the possibility that all things are possible."* – Joseph Chilton Pearce.

Before we can speak of Elder and its wisdom, we must first stand back and look at Elder from a comprehensive view.

Let us begin by focusing on the terms we apply to older humans. All our present terms are negative. Our language matters. When we look at these terms with clear eyes we can see their damage.

We live inside a language-world wherein we have four terms for our older humans: *old,* the *aged, elders,* and *seniors.* None carry a pleasant connotation. For example, it is a compliment to be called young, as in, "Oh, look at the beautiful *young* woman and handsome *young* man." Yet it sounds strange, even bizarre, to hear, "Oh, look at that sexy *old* woman and sexy *old* man."

Old Is Bad

The term *old* lives inside of a dichotomy of good or bad, whereby new is considered good and old is bad, regardless whether we speak of things or people.

The term *aged* may be good for cheese and wine, but it is bad for people. So also is the term *elder.*

With people, all three terms, *old, aged* and *elder* carry an associated meaning of "less than."

The most important term, *Elder,* is scarcely used at all. While it is sometimes used to denote a member of a religious hierarchy, I do not use it in that limited sense.

Further, we dishonor it by writing elder without a capital. To capitalize a word is to honor what the word points to. Grammar books instruct us to capitalize proper nouns, such as our names, thus honoring them. The loss of the capital *E* for *Elder* correlates with the loss of the stage itself. In the long view of human life, Elder had been treated with the honor it deserves.

So I will capitalize it. ***Elder***.

When you see non-capitalized *elder* or *elders,* however, this refers to one or more older people. Both *Elder* and *Elderhood* have long earned their right to capitalization.

Focusing on language is important, for we live our lives inside of language-as-context. When we observe the terms our culture uses, we begin to realize how much we mock, ridicule, and disparage our elders. Further, we live within the pretense that this is *all in fun.*

We Disparage Our Older Adults

The impact of language is profound. I gleaned the following terms from a thesaurus: oldster, old fart, senior, old age as the final stage, old-timer, senescence, dotage, the declining years, over the hill, person of advanced years, winter of life, decrepitude, feebleness, infirmity, superannuated, doddering, senile, along in years, on one's last legs, stricken with years.

I found no terms for Elder that spoke of respect, wisdom or reverence. Absent was any reference to value. All terms pointed either to mental or physical infirmity. The verbal sea we now swim in teems with jagged linguistic seaweed that entraps and drowns our Elders. It makes a mockery of Elderhood.

There is a disconnection between the sad reality of today's widespread disrespect, disempowerment and abandonment of Elder, and the powerful evidence provided by both history and biology for Elder's critical role.

History tells us that Elderhood had been cherished for 99.9 percent of our time on Earth. This is powerful evidence for Elder wisdom as a necessity for the very survival of our human species.

Consider the possibility that Adult, as a stage, might not be wise enough on its own to ensure our survival as a species. Not without the wisdom of Elder. Our present Elder loss represents cultural self-abuse on a worldwide scale.

Ageism Is a Worldwide Phenomenon

Disrespect for Elder is not confined to America. Nor is it just a Western phenomenon.

Susan Collins Marks is Vice President of Search for Common Ground. Susan and her husband John have dedicated their lives to mediating strife in seemingly unworkable areas of the world.

Their highly-respected organization works in the hotspots of four continents, and has made conflict-preventive differences when governments could not. (Check out their website at http://www.SFCG.org).

I asked Susan how the treatment of old people has changed worldwide. She said the spread of ageism was prevalent in the West.

She also told me, "Of course, in the rest of the world, elders are still revered; youth worship is a very Western construct. I am so glad you have taken on this waste of resources and loss to the world of soulful experience."

However, while it might be indeed true that Elders are more revered elsewhere, the trend appears to be downward. A World Health Organization study informs us that both South Africa and China have reported a lack of respect for Elders as underlying their increasing abuse. *(See Notes.)*

In addition, it reported:

"It is generally agreed in these nations (Canada, Lebanon, Kenya, Austria, and Brazil) social values and attitudes of respecting elderly people have changed dramatically for the worse, especially in younger generations. … it is very important to note that disrespect for elderly people is mainly observed in the young…."

This may be due to Western influence. Since the young of today will be the dominant adults of tomorrow, we can expect more disrespect, more ageism.

The Role of Context: It's All in the Setup

Elder lives within a context. And context is crucial.

On a foggy day in 1991, I was traveling with The Hunger Project. Two dozen of us had boarded an ancient steamer from Dakar, Senegal, sailing to Île de Gorée (Gorée Island), the slave-trading island. Millions of slaves had felt the earth of Africa beneath their feet for the last time as they trudged onto the gangplank of the ship-of-horror, to be roughed to the new world in batches, sold; and never saw home again.

While leaning over the rail in the early morning fog, I was approached by Maurice Cohen, a Landmark Seminar Leader from New York City. Standing next to me, he said, apropos of nothing,

"It's all in the setup, Harvey."

"What is, Maurice?"

"Everything!" he replied.

Everything? Yes, everything. As it turns out, I have concluded over the subsequent twenty years the man was right. Everything *is* in the setup. Context is indeed crucial. Context is invisible, yet it is powerful because it contains, allows, and excludes *content.* It is the source of, well, everything. It is not a matter of what we think *about* – that is cont*ent.* Rather, context is where we think *from.*

For example, if you drive 190 miles an hour down the Champs-Elysées, you get handcuffs and a French jail sentence. If you drive that fast in the Indianapolis 500, you get a trophy and two-and-a-half-million dollars. Context is crucial.

As another example, *woman* is a context for a different kind of thinking than occurs within the context *man.* Our native language is a powerful – and limiting – context for our speaking. We think *from* English, or Chinese, or Spanish.

Nesting Contexts

Contexts work like a series of invisible nests, each within the other. Our attitudes and behaviors are influenced by every one of these nests. The inner nest is our *personal* background, attitudes, and points of view.

These in turn lie within the invisible nest of our *family,* which has its own attitudes, approved behaviors, and points of view. These in turn lie within the invisible nest of our particular *culture.* All the different cultures lie, in their turn, within the invisible nest of a worldwide *worldview.*

We could fill in these simple categories with the cultures of a *company,* an *industry,* or a *nation.* Each has its own conversations affecting us as context. Yet these four – personal, family, cultural, and worldview – paint a sufficient picture of the potency of contexts to affect our thinking. And our lives.

Culture as Context

Let's look first at culture as the context for our lives. It is the source of most of our learned behavior. Each of us lives within the context of the attitudes, beliefs, values, standards, ideals, and assumptions our culture imposes.

This context shapes each of us so that we tend to act and respond differently from a person raised in another culture, say, for example, the Mayan culture of 800 AD. Culture as the context for our lives is powerful indeed.

The reason culture is such a powerful control structure is that culture *got here first.* As individuals, we are merely visitors. We are born into our culture, we live inside it, and we will die out of it. The culture goes on.

To use a biologic metaphor, the beehive is the context and the individual bees are the content. Only the hive goes on.

The Power of Our Background Cultural Conversations

These contexts show up as an enormous number of sayings (technically they are called *memes.*) We can speak of the cultural context as a set of conversations that we live inside of. Most conversations we call our own are not our own at all, including the ones we merely think but don't speak.

Our thoughts, in general, are a set of cultural conversations we have not yet put on loudspeaker, rather than our own individual thinking. Yet we believe it is *me* having *my* conversations. Or *me* thinking. But it is more that these conversations belong to the culture and *they have us.* They feel personal … but they aren't.

Think "default." These background conversations determine our lives in the same way the default (background) setting of the Times New Roman font determines how our computer documents look. Our cultural conversations, by default, have our lives look the way they do. These conversations land upon every newborn, are incorporated by each during their life, and continue long beyond their death.

Mostly, they remain invisible and unnoticed. Yet they are powerful beyond measure.

We Are Embedded in Cultural Conversations

> There is an Indian proverb – *"There are three Great Mysteries: Air to the Bird, Water to the Fish and Man to Himself."*

Ah, Man to Himself! Cultural conversations are the context for you and me in the same sense that air is to the bird and water is to the fish, unnoticed but powerfully deterministic. We are *embedded* in them.

Some are true and useful. Some are false and damaging.

Here are a few of the more obviously false: “Tall is better than short.” “Pretty is better than plain.” “Rich is better than poor.” “Slender is better than fat.” “Male is better than female.” “Smart is better than slow.” “Being right is better than being wrong.”

There are many more. The conversation we are most interested in for this book is the following: “Young is better than old.”

My wife, Ellen, walks out onto the porch in the midst of dressing. Her mouth is turned down and she is slumping. “I am having an arm meltdown.” I hold her as she weeps. “No matter how I try, every time I put on a short-sleeved blouse, all I can see is these wrinkles.”

She holds her arms out. The skin hangs and, when she lowers them, multiple wrinkles show up. “See! I know I am almost 70, but …I don’t want to grow old.”

I get caught up. “And I don’t want you to grow old either.” I begin to cry.

She thinks I’m laughing. “Don’t you *laugh* at me!”

“Oh, Sweetheart, I’m not. I’m crying, just like you. I don’t want to grow old either.”

And we cry, loudly and incoherently, for a moment. Then we both start to laugh. We hold each other, now delighted in our being together in our growing-oldness.

The cultural attack is over. Now it is the two of us together, a pair of Elders growing old together.

Culture determines, by default, what we are used to thinking. In other words, we think and speak what our culture says to us.

One way to notice these cultural conversations-into-which-we-were-born is to discern some of the automatic language we use. The term *better than* points to some of these automatic internal conversations. So also do any thoughts containing the terms *should* or *ought to*.

These phrases of our automatic language are yellow flags. They warn us that *what I think* is not actually our own personal thinking. More often it is disguised cultural-think.

We cannot live outside the enormous influence of cultural conversations. However, it is possible, with work, to step outside them sufficiently to identify many of our inherited conversational webs.

Then we can notice our automatic imprisonment. Identifying these will become important when we speak about training ourselves to become Elders.

Again, we are what the culture says we are.

Unless we question it.

Elders question it.

Correlation: Conversations and Actions Correlate

We like to think our actions and what we speak are considered and deliberate. This is rarely so. Usually they are as automatic as the knee that jerked when I tapped upon the patellar tendon during my rotation through neurology. Tap-jerk. Our internal conversations and our actions (including speaking) are so linked as to correlate as tightly as the knee jerk.

All actions are preceded by an internal conversation, even as short as "Bee!" Jump! The thought of *bee* and the action of *jump* are so tightly entwined as to be one thing – *beejump!*

Here's why. Consider the First Law of Performance – *How people perform correlates to how situations occur to them.* The Second Law says, *How a situation occurs arises in language.* ("Bee!")

This law informs us that we can only make sense of another's actions if we knew how the situation occurred for her. Then the action she took would make perfect sense to us.

Regarding our older people, these first two Laws of Performance inform us that the treatment of our elders (performance) correlates with *the way elders occur for us.* And our cultural conversation about them is thus crucial, because our actions follow those conversations as night follows day. When our language for our elders is that they are "less than," so too we treat them.

These two laws, and the third, are presented powerfully by Steve Zaffron and Dave Logan in their 2009 book, *The Three Laws of Performance.*

Our Background Conversations: Old Is Not As Good As Young

While cultural conversations impact each of us, sometimes harshly, let's focus on one that bears directly on the topic of Elder.

If this is not obvious at first, the television ads for products to make us look prettier (this means younger), sexier (younger), and more virile (younger) are. Have you ever seen an advertisement promoting the concept of looking older? In the advertising world, a microcosm of our culture, youth sells. Old does not.

False Assumption

The assumption that old is not as good as young is a lie.

Old offers more value than young. However, this is risky ground because saying *more* sets up an either/or dichotomy and I prefer not to do that. Rather, it is more useful to acknowledge the old as more experienced than the young. And experience *means* something, for it is a precursor to wisdom. It is not enough, but it is a beginning.

The old have experienced more. They have had a longer time living on this planet to garner insight. They have made more mistakes than the young. The old have observed more success and failure and seen more changes than the young.

For example, no young person today lived through the Great Depression of the 1930s. Those hard times impacted people deeply. The young might read about it, but they cannot experience what it was like for a family to roam from town to town looking for work, shelter, and food, carrying only a few possessions from their previous life.

Old has seen more patterns play out than the young. Old has been exposed to a greater variety of human beings and a larger variety of human experiences than the young. And old has had more opportunities to express love.

Further, the old are more likely to have learned humility, a rare quality in the young. In short, the old have been around the block and the young have not. And that experience has great value.

While these traits do not make the old better, Elders have earned a higher place on the *natural hierarchy of life progression* than the young.

The Realism of a Declining Body

Let's pause for a moment to be realistic. What about the physical aging of the body? Regarding becoming Elder, it simply doesn't matter. Obviously, we will all die. And we may become infirm first.

Elder knows and includes this. Living long to become an Elder brings bodily changes with it. So what? After all, Elderhood is not a game of soccer that demands a strong body. It is a much bigger game.

Elder is not an age of life, rather it is a stage of life. It is a way of being. And it is a way of being by *choice.* Each of us has the choice whether to focus on the declining body, or focus on the upsurge of spirit that Elder can exhibit.

Sidebar

John Robbins, author of six books, spoke of the creativity of elders. He referred to his good friend Laura Huxley, author, film producer and widow of Aldous Huxley, the famous English writer and philosopher.

Laura loved hiking and into her nineties would still hike alone in the hills. However, her eyesight deteriorated to the point where she was afraid she might get lost. So she got a treadmill. She lived alone and often worked around the house in the nude.

Robbins tells of the day he knocked on her door. She apparently did not hear him. So, being the sort of friend who could simply walk in, he did so. And saw her in her fullness – nude, dancing on the treadmill, and singing at full voice. Laura was ninety-four.

Robbins said he was struck by how alive she was, and how expressive. He concluded, "Now *that* was creative. So when something is lost, put in something else to replace it!"

The Role of Perception in Aging

A decades-long study by Becca Levy concludes that the perception of aging is critical to health. Those who had positive views and perceptions of aging not only had less distress in the present than those with negative perceptions of growing older, but they actually lived longer.

Levy, the primary author, concluded that when elderly persons are prompted to view themselves as senile, they experience compromised memory performance, decreased will to live, poor cardiovascular response to stress, and negative views of older people.

By contrast, those with more positive self-perceptions of aging had an increase in all markers including an additional seven-and-a-half years of life. This was more than the longevity gained from having low blood pressure, low cholesterol, maintaining a healthy weight, abstaining from smoking, or from exercising regularly.

You can find the study located at the website http://www.ncbi.nlm.nih.gov. *Journal of Personality and Social Psychology* (Vol. 83, No. 2, pp. 261-70).

It becomes clear that if you take the stand that you *are* a wise Elder, you will live as one. And if you take the stand you are becoming senile, you will have that experience instead.

Our beliefs matter.

Two Worldviews

Remembering Bucky's comments about finding the trimtab to alter humanity's course, I continually asked myself where the trimtab was. My version was to live inside this question, "Where is the trimtab located so that I might, with others, move it and co-create a great future for humanity?"

What I have realized is something very basic. The future for humanity rests solidly upon its worldview.

Every one of us has a *view of the world.* I will refer to this as our *worldview*. Worldviews function as a set of guidelines, a map that informs us how the world works.

Our *individual* worldview contains the attitudes, opinions, and assumptions that each of us – as individuals – make about ourselves, others, and life itself. To amplify what I wrote earlier, we each have a worldview about ourselves (whether I am good or bad), about others (whether they like me or dislike me, whether they are trustworthy or not), and about life (whether it is safe or unsafe).

While each of us has his or her individual worldview, there is also a composite worldview of a culture shared by all members. It is built into each culture. Further, by synthesizing the worldview of all cultures, we can notice that there is a worldview all humans have in common, a *worldwide* worldview. I will call this worldwide-worldview-in-common … simply, *our worldview.*

Our worldview is shared by every human being and it is the most basic context for every human being. The examination of worldviews lies within the province of ontology, the study of *being*. Think of worldview as the most basic *given* of being human. Worldview has a “Well, of course, obviously” tone.

Context, expressed at the level of worldview, has vast implications for human beings. Not only for our present times, but also in the analysis of the past.

The most basic history of the world is the history of shifting worldviews.

Most importantly, our worldview is the bedrock of the future. The future of our planet and our species. The future of our world will correlate to our underlying worldview.

The You *AND* Me Worldview

Let’s examine what the inclusive worldview of You AND Me might look like. Such a worldview is inherent within our *universal desire* for our grandchildren and our grandchildren’s grandchildren to live in a world better than the one we live in.

The You AND Me worldview doesn’t leave anybody out. After all, do we not all yearn for a world where every child feels loved and safe? A world where all kids have enough food and shelter and clothing? A world where every child has the opportunity to be fully self-expressive with the opportunity to fulfill their life’s purpose?

Such a future would be based on a worldview of connection, inclusion, and love.

At our deepest level of being human, we want a future that works for everyone, with no one left out. It is the obvious worldview when we contemplate, with fresh eyes, that magnificent photo of our beautiful blue and white and green planet, our Earth hanging in space.

No boundaries can be seen, for there are none except those made by humans. Viewing the planet from afar in this way, we are able to see that we are indeed the crew of our very own Spaceship Earth. We can also sense that this is IT and we are ONE.

This is the essence of the worldview of You AND Me.

Using the phrase You AND Me is awkward. Let's refer to it simply as the AND worldview.

The worldview of AND arises naturally from the deep inner knowing we are all one humanity. It means we walk in each other's shoes. At our biologic core, we are herd animals – if you think of a human herd as a tribe, a village. Our basic social unit is tribe.

The AND worldview implies that I only make it if you do. AND means if you don't make it, I don't either because the unit is the tribe. Within tribe, even if that tribe is the entire human species, the worldview is still – AND.

This worldview recognizes the deep, permanent and profound bond between all humans, and between all living things. It is the worldwide expansion of the famous declaration of the Four Musketeers, "All for One and One for All!" It is a worldview of cooperation, mutual interdependency, caring, and compassion.

"In a world that is round, it doesn't make sense to take sides," says Dr. Arleen Pitcock Bump, Spiritual Director of the Center of Spiritual Living in Fort Lauderdale. Dr. Bump has suggested that the AND worldview could also be called, You AS Me.

Reverend Philip Elton Collins, a spiritual channel and author, uses the term "*We* Consciousness." He contrasts it with our present "*Me* Consciousness." Albert Einstein also endorsed this concept in a 1937 letter to American artist Max Bohm:

"A human being is a part of the whole called by us, 'Universe,' a part limited in time and space. He experiences himself, his thoughts and feelings as something separated from the rest … a kind of optical delusion of his consciousness.

"This delusion is a kind of prison for us, restricting us to our personal desires and to the affections for a few people nearest to us. Our task must be to free ourselves from this prison by widening our circle of compassion to embrace all living creatures and the whole nature in its beauty."

Darwin Smartened Up

Charles Darwin realized the AND of the natural world. He became so impressed with *cooperation and interdependence* as the basic relationship between species, he wrote extensively of this in his second book, *The Descent of Man.*

The observations he made as a more mature scientist caused him to theorize that the most successful species were not, as he had originally thought, a function of "survival of the fittest." Upon deeper examination, he came to believe that successful survival was a function of *cooperation,* both within species and between species.

Microcosms and Macrocosms. Is 'AND' a Cosmic Law?

At the level of *human body,* we are made up several trillion cells, each of which is a cooperative entity. Biologists tell us the human body has about *7000 times* more cells than the Earth has humans. In that sense, our planet is oddly tiny compared to a single human being.

At the *planetary* level, our planet can be thought of as a single entity made up of more than seven billion humans. Each of us can be seen as a cooperative walking-around-and-interacting cell.

The AND worldview is vast and inclusionary. It may turn out to be even greater than just a worldview. It might be one of the most basic Laws of Creation. Some cosmologists believe that, at the level the cosmos, our Earth is akin to the cell in a galaxy. Galaxies, in their turn, may be cells in the body of the universe.

Peter Russell, author of *From Science to God: A Physicist's Journey into the Mystery of Consciousness,* wrote this to me:

> *"And possibly as many more Universes beyond as there are stars in this one. Mind-boggling hardly touches it."*

Traveling deep into the depths of the microcosm, we can see that the cells in our body have interdependency down pat. Each cell works with other cells to do the work of an organ, and each organ works in concert with other organs to create a functioning human body.

Each organ works in a way that demonstrates, *Hey, we are an US!* And each cell in each organ cooperates to demonstrate that *Hey, we are also an US!*

It seems clear to me that, just as our cells live inside the worldview of AND, so do our organs. The organs all work together, and that makes the body function properly. Can you imagine how bad it would be if your pancreas went to war with your spleen?

Traveling deeper into the depths of the microcosm, life continues to demonstrate cooperation and interdependence. The AND worldview exists at the subcellular level, at the level of DNA molecules, within atoms, and to the quantum subatomic level.

Scientists have shown that the conditions of cooperation and interdependence exist in abundance at the most micro levels of known life.

It is AND all the way, from bottom to top and from top to bottom.

How hard is it then to imagine that we humans have been *evolutionarily designed* to live within this worldview? Might we humans develop enough wisdom to act in a collective manner that demonstrates that *WE too are an US?*

Might we possibly evolve enough to function as an *interdependent* whole, an *integrated* whole, within the natural *worldview* of You AND Me?

Perhaps such an insight is inherent within us, existing deep in our inherited human knowingness. This nursery rhyme by the mathematician August de Morgan is from 150 years ago, yet it hints at such an awareness.

Big fleas have little fleas,
Upon their backs to bite 'em,
And little fleas have lesser fleas,
And so, ad infinitum.

And the great fleas, themselves, in turn
Have greater fleas to go on;
While these again have greater still,
And greater still, and so on.

Natural Way of the Universe

The very size of human beings is interesting. Human beings are exactly *halfway* on the scale between the tiniest unit of the microcosm – Planck's

Constant – and the largest unit of the macrocosm, the universe itself.

Joel Primack, professor of physics and astrophysics at the University of Southern California, says, "The size of a human being is at the center of all the possible sizes in the universe.... Sixty orders of magnitude separate the very smallest (ten to the minus 30th) from the very largest (ten to the plus 30th). We are in the exact middle."

Coincidence? Perhaps. I find it strongly suggestive that not only is the worldview of AND *possible,* but the ultimate *goal* for humanity is to live within this worldview, just as does the rest of the universe, large and small.

The You *OR* Me Worldview

What about the condition of our present world? Clearly, we do not live in an AND world. Rather, we live inside a worldview of You OR Me thinking.

While games and athletic contests are, technically, in this category, I am not speaking of these, for they are agreed-upon games with rules defining merely temporary "winners" or "losers." Rather we are speaking of huge systems of ritualized disparity existing over time.

We live in a world where there are vast inequalities, a world where huge groups of people have been left out.

We live inside a patriarchal system which has demoted, diminished, and sidelined women. Thousands of books and articles attest to the seriousness of sexism.

All the *isms* in our world of today are the result of the thinking humans have done to date – racism, sexism, and ageism, to name a few. These plagues are all the natural byproducts of our present OR worldview.

The Assumption of Scarcity

There are two basic assumptions that underlie the worldview of OR. The first of these is the Assumption of Scarcity, the supposition that the necessities of life are scarce.

The OR thinking proceeds automatically. "Survival of me, or whatever I consider myself to be (my family, my tribe, my nation), is threatened if I do not get what I need. I believe that what I need is scarce, so I must prevent *you* from getting what you need."

In summary, "I must win and you must lose."

When situations occur like this, all actions correlate to it. Out of this and its correlated actions, comes the world as we know it – societies and nations in competition, often warlike, with each other.

This world of OR is solidified by the second assumption.

The Assumption of Disconnection

This assumption states we are all independent entities, that there is no spiritual connection between me and you and other humans, and certainly no connection between me and other living entities, plants or animals. The assumption declares with vehemence, "I am *not* you!"

The OR worldview is known as a zero-sum game, one where there are major losers and apparent winners. This is the worldview of today.

Neither of the two assumptions underlying the OR worldview are valid. They are both false. In fact, we are all connected by a bond. All life is an inseparable whole, and each living entity consists, at its quantum base, as energy.

While each entity may appear distinct, as when the index finger gazes at the thumb, yet there is the hand that connects them. Nothing is a disconnected entity in our interconnected universe, even though the connection may not be apparent to us with our limited view. We humans are, by our very nature, interconnected herd animals, tribal animals.

Nor are there *inherent* scarcities in the world. There is enough food, there is enough water, and there is enough shelter for everyone. Moreover, these are not even the real necessities for life. And there is an abundance of the real necessities – caring, love, imagination, compassion, kindness, freedom and possibility.

These exist in vast profusion, regardless of whether we choose to perceive their presence. They are present for each of us if we say so; they are only absent if we say they are absent.

Summary

Albert Einstein once said, "The world we have today is a direct correlate of the thinking mankind has done to date." He also said, "It cannot be changed without changing our thinking."

Almost a hundred years later, I would paraphrase his words – *Our world cannot be changed without transforming our worldview from You OR Me to You AND Me.*

Loss of Elder

There are enormous losers within the OR worldview … notably women, the non-white, and the poor. One of the most dangerous byproducts of this worldview is the loss of our Third Stage of Life. To be old in our modern world is to be considered *less than.* Instead of Elderhood being an opportunity for adventure, contribution and respect, it is dreaded. The term Elder has devolved to a label of disrespect. In twenty-first century America specifically and in Western culture generally, to be old is to be disempowered.

What Elder Is Now

Let us first look at the present condition of Elder. Then we can examine how Elder has devolved from its honored status to its present trivial position.

Our views of life live inside the conversations of our culture. These cultural conversations can often be spotted by listening both to the conversations of others and to our own self-talk. Remember, our cultural conversations are mirrored by our inner ones that we think are uniquely our own, but are not. Rather, each of our inner conversations with ourselves (self-talk) is a mirror version of the larger cultural dialogue.

The FOREGROUND Conversation of Our Culture

There is a foreground conversation how the culture speaks to its old:

> *"You've done your time. You don't have to do it any longer. We will relieve you of your burdens. Thank you for your efforts. Enjoy your retirement."*

While this sounds both kindly and altruistic, something else is unspoken in the background, something ugly and hypocritical.

From time to time, an older person becomes clear about our diminished state. Personally, I would be indignant. If I were to remove restraint and turn up the volume, my indignation might sound like this:

> "This is monstrous! We who have contributed so much, helped society, paid taxes, raised families, contributed to the growth of the economy, of the nation – have been put out to pasture? We are being told to spend the rest of our lives in leisure? No! I don't want to be told to go relax, join a book club, play bridge or golf."

I am insulted when the culture says:

> *"After all, Compulsory Retirement is our gift to you for a life well lived. Why can't you just sit back and smell the*

> *roses? Or go get a travel trailer and hang out with the other retirees?"*
>
> "How dare you! Why should I? I have trained myself, put myself into action, done important things. I have produced, I have sacrificed. And now, just when I have finally attained my greatest level of competence, you pat me on the head condescendingly and throw me away?"

The culture responds:

> *"Okay, so we'll throw you a bone. You are now a Senior Citizen. Congratulations!"*

This kind of talk, mostly unspoken, angers me. I am not stupid. I have been around the block and I'm street smart. I know what *senior citizen* means. It means second class. So I might retort,

> "Hey, listen. I have so much more to offer, to the culture, to our children, the community, the world. Yet, the system is set up to bribe me with small nothings. A pension – which I earned! And a discount at the movies! Well, whoopee damn doo!"

The Background Conversation of Our Culture

Culture's responses point to the depth, and danger, in culture's background conversation. It includes the mocking:

"Don't get too disorderly, now, old person. Just sit quietly in your rocking chair. We are going to laugh at you and make fun of all your objections anyway.

"And don't make us snicker by wearing youthful clothes or trying in any way to make yourself look young like us or we will have your children tell you that you look ridiculous. We will make fun of you behind your back. 'Can you believe it? She had her nose pierced and she's almost 70!' To your face, we might ask, 'Hey, wanna hear a really great joke about old farts? It's hilarious!' "

There might be threatening:

"Move over, old person. It's our turn now. We want the power. You've had it long enough. You've messed up your children, your families, and your institutions. Just look at the state of the economy, education, the environment, politics.

"It's your generation's fault we're in such a mess. Now we have to fix it. We don't want to spend any more money to support your uselessness. Things are tough and we can't afford it (you)."

Should we fail to follow Adult's rules of how we should behave, we are guided into special communities, exclusive ones too, just for us *senior citizens*. If we persist in our self-expression and make waves, then we are moved to retirement homes, nursing homes, mental institutions.

Or we get shoved into the back bedrooms of our reluctant children, who are forced to hire the untrained and out of work to take care of the old person who has become a problem. A burden.

The old person is kept out of sight, out of mind. And soon enough *out of their mind.*

Ageism

The term for this type of background conversation is ageism. *Wikipedia* says it well, in words that are down and dirty: "Ageism is the stereotyping and discriminating against individuals or groups on the basis of their age. The term is patterned on sexism and racism. It includes prejudicial attitudes towards old age and even to the aging process itself."

Ageism is the doctrine that holds that one stage of life is superior to another. We live inside the background assumption that to be 30 is better than to be 70 or 80 or, God Forbid, 90. We don't just *believe* that this is so. We *know* it is so. And this *knowing* is insidious, unconscious and pervades all our thinking and speaking.

Ageism is fear-based. It may be overt and obvious, taking virulent forms including job exclusion and forced retirement. Or it may show up as covert, often expressed in so-called humor that depicts older people as helpless, useless, or foolish. Ageism includes an unconscious, emotional reaction of distaste and a desire to exclude oneself from the company of older people.

There is considerable evidence of discrimination against the elderly in healthcare settings. In the patient-physician interaction, physicians and other healthcare providers may hold attitudes that are ageist, discriminating against older patients.

Studies have found some physicians do not show concern about the medical problems of older people.

While interacting with older patients, doctors may view them with disgust and describe them in negative ways such as *depressed* or *crazy*. Elderly people are less likely than younger people to be screened for cancers so are less likely to be diagnosed at early stages.

Ageism has significant effects on elderly people. The stereotyping and infantilizing of older people by patronizing language diminishes self-esteem and causes changes in behavior. Studies have shown when people hear stereotypes about their supposed incompetence and uselessness, they perform worse on measures of competence and memory.

The stereotypes become self-fulfilling prophesies.

We Are Colluders

However, we Elders cannot avoid our own role in the situation. We participate with our oppressors in the same way that the victimized dance the dance of collusion with those who victimize them. Muggers and muggees, for example, *arise together*. For example, *"What was I thinking that I would walk alone in that bad neighborhood at 2 a.m.?"*

Taking ownership for our actions eliminates victimhood. Taking responsibility for our part in the dance provides power. As in the mugger/muggee scenario, cultural ageism and we as colluders, have *risen together*.

Rising Together

I find it useful to consider our present condition of ageism to be without fault and without blame. I am reluctant to use the terms “caused by” or “resulting from.” It is not useful to attempt to assign blame, for in my view there is no blame to be assigned. I prefer the idea of *correlation,* which also means *rising together.* The core of this thinking is, “Things are the way they are because things are the way they are.” This view allows correlation and eliminates blame.

Thus we can say that ageism has arisen quite naturally out of our deepest background conversation – our worldview of OR. Now we can speak of ageism having “risen together” with industrialization. It has also risen together with the development of cities, with our longer life span, and with the revolution in technology.

Ageism is dangerous and is powerful and it is a phenomenon that we need to reckon with. It is particularly dangerous because our present culture, Youth, Adult and Elders alike, have bought into it, regardless of the fact that our buying-in has been unconscious. Ageism shows up hourly and daily in our thinking and in our speaking.

Subtle Ageism

Let’s use humor as an example. There are many aging jokes to be found on the Internet. Some are amusing, but underneath the humor they all have a similar message: *our elders are less than us.*

For example:

The older I get, the better I was.
Age is important only if you're cheese or wine.
Seen it all, done it all, can't remember most of it.
Once over the hill, you pick up speed.

Recently I looked for a birthday card for a friend around my age. Many of the cards were blatantly ageist, pretending at humor. I was struck by the lack of dignity these cards expressed. I am not suggesting that old people jokes are always bad, but note that we no longer see cards poking fun at race, creed, and sexual orientation.

So why, we might ask, is everyone still cracking ageism jokes? Because we have been able *to get away with it.* And obviously because they are funny. But they're funny only for the mind that is fertile ground for such humor. And that mind is *our* mind, for we are afraid, even terrified, of growing old. So we joke about it.

However, such jokes do not ease our minds about aging. The negativity associated with getting old has become insidious. Perhaps, just perhaps, this kind of thinking might result in us getting old faster.

Elders Mocked on TV

Old people are often the butt of humor for television comedians. Our culture has grown up just enough so comedians no longer tell racist jokes. Instead, they have come up with another easy target to diminish and deprecate – Elders. The tongue-in-cheek delivery is designed to assure us it is "all in good fun, of course."

It is not.

Fear of the Other

Ageist jokes are more subtle than the horrendous racist jokes of years ago. In those days, we were fueled by fear of the stranger, particularly one with black skin. But the fear then was, for most, a *potential* fear. The dark skin was *over there,* removed from us as a whole. Yet the jokes were pervasive and damaging.

During my teens in my small lily-white New England town, I did not know a single black person. However the racist jokes were rampant, along with jokes about other ethnic groups. We told n….. jokes, cracked lines about wops, spics, the Portagee, and the little moron. We were afraid of anyone unfamiliar, anyone different than us, so we joked to keep ourselves feeling superior and safe.

The fear of getting old is more real. It is immediate and pertinent to all of us because aging is universal and inevitable, rather than just potential. For anyone who is afraid of dying, old age is fearful indeed, fertile ground for such humor.

Where Went Courage?

Elders can fight back. We must discover the courage to stand up and object to cheap humor that insults and degrades us. Instead, like tamed sheep we gather around to laugh at our very old, our grandmothers and grandfathers. Meanwhile, today's popular comedians diminish their wisdom, insight, kindness, and concern about becoming a burden to others – into foolishness.

All our future generations will become elders one day, and they will not look back at us kindly. We would better serve them (our children, grandchildren and great-grandchildren) if we made conscious, now, the pernicious ageism that insults and demeans us. Perhaps it is our *duty* to restore Elder to that most honored of our three life stages.

Elders Have Our Own Conversations

It is not just "them."

Elders have our own *foreground* conversations (the content we speak out loud) and our own *background* conversations (the context, where we speak from).

A typical foreground conversation might sound like this:

"I am so glad to finally have the children out and on their own. Free, free at last! And I love it here in Florida. No more cold winters. Oh, look what those fools are doing in Congress. They fight, accomplish nothing. I hate politics, I'd rather play bridge. The club meets twice a week and we have an important tournament coming up.

"My husband just loves going fishing and playing golf. Or is it bowling? I think the kids are coming for Christmas this year. They couldn't make it last year because the grandchildren were caught up in their school activities and sports. Still, I am just so happy to be retired. No, really, I am."

However, the *background* conversation may sound more like this:

"I am so tired. I really need to go to the doctor to find out if there's something wrong with me. I miss my friends. I wonder how they're doing back at the office. Yeah, that movie last night was okay, but nothing like the classics we used to see.

"I wonder why Ruthie didn't call like she said she would. And Jim just up and died? We didn't even hear about it until three days after the funeral. Boy, they better not cremate me. I just read the average person spends four hours a day watching television. That's terrible, but then again, I've had the TV on all day today. I can't believe it's Billie's seventy-fifth birthday tomorrow.

"I wonder when the kids are going to call. Don't they know one of the Ten Commandments is to "Honor Thy Father and Mother"? They visit so rarely and they never ask me my opinion on anything anymore. I barely know what's going on in their lives."

Gates Slam Shut

Just when older adults have become most knowledgeable and most competent, we are told our time is over. Just when we are about to pass through the gates of wisdom, the gates are slammed shut. In the denial of our rightful passage into Elder status, we have been relegated to merely getting old. There is no longer a rightful passage into Elderhood: there is no longer an Elderhood to enter.

The Western culture is an adolescent culture, one that has forgotten that impressive distinction of Elder. Few of us retain any personal memory of the honor once respectfully bestowed upon the white-haired, the people who had lived long and experienced much in life.

We have forgotten to honor those in the culture who learned by living, who became both compassionate and wise with the years, who could act as transmitters of individual and cultural wisdom.

Ageism is repressive. Such repression of the human spirit results in lives of quiet desperation, waste of human potential, and the sadness of unfulfilled dreams.

Ageism is not limited to America. Ageism abounds wherever America has influence. Once again, Thoreau's quote: "Most men lead lives of quiet desperation and go to the grave with their song still in them."

Or, as the British philosopher Alan Watts explained in more crude terms, "As we grow older our world shrinks so much that by the very end, we have become as a tube, with great interest about what we put in one end and take out the other."

How Did Elder Get Lost?

I will share my own view of elder lost via a short basic history, a story of worldviews.

Long ago, Elders were honored. No campfire was held without us. No talking stick passed us by. We were called Grandmother and Grandfather and we were beloved for our knowledge and wisdom. Called upon to be wise, we responded and brought forth wisdom from our connection with Spirit.

This is how it was for thousands of lifetimes, vast generations where life was lived as one's forbearers had. Elders were intelligent and created lives of joy, full of dancing, relationship and love for one another. Elders embodied the wisdom that bridged thousands of generations. We were the bibles of ongoing life for the tribe.

We humans were born of the earth, we loved the earth and when old we returned our bodies to the earth. Our spirits returned to the Great Spirit, our true home. There we prepared to return again.

Earth was good and we were as other species, we two-leggers. And we loved and appreciated the four-leggers and the eight-leggers and the no-leggers. All was one and we were a part of the One. Our muscles were our energy, our love was our energy, and our warmth came from the sun and from wood. We thrived by keeping our numbers in check so the good Earth could take care of us all and so we could take care of our mother, our good Earth. We lived rightly.

We knew in our bones who we were and who our children were and who our great-great-grandparents were for fifteen generations back. We were born, we lived and we died in a great partnership with the Earth, with the sun and the moon, with each other, and with every other species that loved us and took care of us. And we loved them in return.

We lived within the inclusive world of AND.

Things Began to Change

The change was slow at first. And we did not notice, for the change took generations. We began to gather in larger groups and we began to specialize in work. No longer did every family hunt and gather and move with the seasons or food source. Instead, we built more permanent settlements, larger and larger in size, first towns, then cities.

Our fields were farther from our central gathering place. So we gathered together less often for celebrations. We became spread out, distant from one another.

At first this was not a problem for Elders, because our young remembered to value and honor us. We were valuable to them.

From Horticulture to Agrarian

Over the centuries, our built-in natural cooperation shifted into competition as money came into existence and commerce became more important. Around 5000 years ago, we also changed from a horticultural society with a food production system beyond the hunter-gatherer mode, whereby digging sticks were used to cultivate small gardens, to a more advanced agrarian society.

Our economy was based on producing and maintaining farmland. Cultivating land was the primary source of wealth and required technological advances to produce crops over a large area.

Ken Wilbur, founder of Integral Theory, has pointed out that "within a horticultural society, exemplified as a [family] planting done via a 'woman with a hoe,' woman was honored. But when we shifted to the agrarian society of 'man with a horse and a plow,' their greater strength allowed men the ascendency."

Patriarchy Began

Around this time, man began to develop overriding importance in the culture, particularly the young and strong man, while women were regarded as being less important.

With the rise in the social structure of man over woman, commonly called the patriarchy, came a terrible loss.

This was felt most deeply by women, especially the wise old woman once respectfully and affectionately known as the *crone.* Eventually the term *crone* became one of disrespect. Women suffered and elders, both men and women, began to suffer from the dismissal of their wisdom.

For a few thousand years, Elders, primarily men, still held the respect of the people. Many wise Elders continued as teachers, statesmen, heads of churches, and heads of governments.

The rest continued working as small farmers, each family with enough land and wisdom to raise crops to feed themselves, generation upon generation. We traded our abundance in the marketplaces for handmade specialized goods. Life went on much as usual, with most of us still deeply connected to the land and to the seasons. We remained aware of our inseparability from the earth.

Elders were still the repository of history, wisdom, guidance, the old ways that worked, the stories of our oneness with Spirit. Elders continued to be the walking Bibles of Life.

Shift in Worldview from AND to OR

Human beings still lived within the deep understanding of All as Spirit. Their worldview of relationship was based on the AND worldview that included all living things. The Lakota Sioux had a term for this: *Aho Mitakuye Oyasin,* meaning: “All our relations” or “We are all related.”

The move into towns and cities was accompanied by an emerging worldview. This worldview began to supersede the deeply personal You AND Me worldview.

We became less inclusive and less connected to nature. Over time, humanity shifted into the competitive worldview of You OR Me.

Towns and cities had great advantages to commerce and safety, but they also assumed a major liability with the inability to migrate. When a tribe developed critical shortages, everyone simply migrated to an area of abundance. Towns and cities, however, couldn't move whenever shortages occurred.

Loss of Energy Sources

Arnold Toynbee, the widely-respected British historian and philosopher, studied twenty-one major civilizations, all extinct.

His studies and others showed that as a civilization expanded, it eventually grew beyond one or more of the three required sources of energy – food and water resources, fuel for cooking and warmth, and work energy by means of oxen, horses, or manpower (often slaves).

When an energy source became scarce, a civilization had to locate other resources in order to survive. This threat of extinction spurred expansion into territories of others, often resulting in war.

The historical cooperative worldview of AND shifted to the competitive OR worldview.

The Essence of the OR Worldview

This new worldview of OR made sense for those times. Recall that the bottom line in this worldview of insufficiency and disconnection is that *I must get what I need and prevent you from getting what you need.* It shows up as a zero-sum game, *I must win and you must lose.*

Such thinking put all of us in competition with each other. Our universal connection became lost. No longer did we experience being connected to each other, to the Earth, to Spirit. Rather we became attuned to a pair of antagonistic distinctions – *us* and those *others.* Those *others* became a threat … other tribes, other nations, and eventually everyone else. Strangers (not us) became non-people and could be treated as mere objects. Profoundly dehumanizing, this led to seeing ourselves as separate entities. We competed, often ferociously, for whatever we perceived as scarce and necessary.

This is the very essence of the OR worldview.

And it continues to be our worldview today. Sadly, we have not, at our most basic and unconscious level, evolved significantly from when we created our earliest towns and city-states.

Fossil Fuels

The competitive OR worldview took a sudden leap 200 years ago, beginning with the discovery of a novel source of energy – fossil fuels. I call that period of early use the *Energy Leap.* We have used that grand and one-time gift from the earth to develop marvelous technologies to both extend our lifetimes and to have our longer lives be more comfortable.

Yet for every gift, there is price to be paid by someone. If not by us, then the price must be paid by our descendants. For, as the profound expression explains, "There ain't no free lunch!"

Paradox

So today we live in a strife-filled world as isolated and disconnected individual entities, gathered reluctantly into groups without profound affiliation. Yet at the same time, we have become technologically advanced.

We have also created, for the first time in the history of the world, the means to totally destroy our own species. This is perhaps our saddest achievement. Such a tragic paradox.

Can We? Should We?

We have created the means to destroy ourselves. Now the biggest question humanity faces is *whether we have the wisdom to refrain from doing so.*

Adult, our dominant stage, tends to live in the immediate question, "What *can* we do; what *can* we build?" Elder, wiser, looks down the road for generations and asks "But *should* we?" Perhaps with the loss of Elder we have ceased to be *humane becomings,* a term coined by Don Pet, M.D. Instead, we have regressed, at our poorest, to mere *human doings.*

Evolutionary Downstep

Consider the possibility that we have not only stunted our emotional and spiritual evolution, but we humans may have *devolved.* By adopting the OR worldview, we might have taken an evolutionary downstep. We may be on that road more easily traveled, to the detriment of our planet and all the species who call it home, including us humans.

Would this have happened had we been wiser? If we had retained the institution of Elder?

Perhaps not.

Correlation, Not Causation

In this evaluation, we must be careful not to become lost in causation. Causation (cause and effect) is often not as useful a concept as correlation. There is a critical difference in thinking. We have touched upon correlation previously, but it needs expansion.

Consider a dog. Dogs have heads and dogs have tails. The head does not cause the tail nor does the tail cause the head. Rather they correlate.

Apply this to the loss of Elder. We cannot say that the loss was *because of* fossil fuels, population growth, or the industrial revolution. Although all arose over roughly the same period, we cannot say that any one of these *caused* the others.

Rather, they all arose together in correlation with the shift in humanity's most basic outlook – from its ancient, tried and true worldview of AND to its present discordant worldview of OR.

The AND worldview was the prevalent worldview for untold thousands of generations. Only for the last eight generations has the shift to OR begun to alter humanity's most basic social unit – family.

The Energy Leap – Oil

As I wrote earlier, the world transformed almost exactly 200 years ago with the discovery of fossil fuels. The Energy Leap is when everything dramatically shifted, only eight generations ago. Almost immediately the human population (less than 750 million) began to soar.

Our present world population is 7.3 billion people. This is *a tenfold increase in the blink of the evolutionary eye.*

Sidebar

At the dawn of agriculture, about 6000 BC, the population of the world is estimated at five million. At the time of Jesus, the world population had gradually crept to 200 million. It took all of human history for the world population to reach one billion.

A tremendous change occurred with the discovery of fossil fuels.

- A second billion was achieved in only 123 years (1927)
- The third in 33 years (1960)
- The fourth in 14 years (1974)
- The fifth in 13 years (1987)
- The sixth in12 years (1999)
- The seventh billion in 10 years (2011)
- As of October 2015, the world population is 7.3 billion.

How big a gift is oil? A single barrel of crude oil weighing 320 pounds is equivalent to the energy of one large man working eight hours a day, forty hours per week, for more than eleven years. At an hourly wage of $22, the energy in a barrel of crude is worth $500,000. A fifty-dollar barrel of crude oil can produce *a half million dollars of work.* This is a ratio of 10,000 to one.

Thus far, fossil fuels have been the gift that keeps on giving. The question is, for how much longer?

Suddenly, we no longer needed horsepower, muscle power, slave power, or wood power. Oil, coal, and natural gas enabled the development of fertilizers, new building materials, plastics with multiple properties, and the web of global communication that eventually culminated in the Internet.

The Global Brain

The web of communication has been called the Global Brain. We are now connected by technology. The thick cloak of information surrounding our planet into which we can tap is known as the *noosphere* (pronounced *noo′-oh-sfere*), or the sphere of human thought.

As a tiny example, I can look at my smart phone and can instantly find out the weather in Hong Kong or Paris.

Our worldwide connectivity allows us to know what is happening everywhere on our planet. However, our technological interconnectivity has also contributed to our disconnection. As speaking in depth has declined, texting has soared.

Communication has increased in breadth, but lost its depth.

We Lost Elder When Elder Became Superfluous

There is another way to look at Elder loss. Elder became superfluous to the needs of the culture. At least to the needs *as perceived by Adults.*

Adult, the oldest form of Youth, has become committed to power and accumulation and, in its arrogance, has refused to accept the wisdom of the Elder.

This is understandable when we consider that the world of Adult – the world of technology, of mass communication – had begun to move so fast that Adult no longer believed old people had a significant contribution to make. The wisdom of the Elder was seen as outdated and of another time.

Under the sway of the Adult cry of "Progress! Progress!" Elder advice was no longer attended. Self-doubting, Elder faded away and, eventually, gave up.

Cult of Adulthood

Dr. William H. Thomas has offered an insightful analysis that makes a great deal of sense. He says our Western culture, under the influence of the vast numbers of Baby Boomers, has developed a *cult* of adulthood.

Regarding *cult,* Carole Kammen, the founder of the Pathways Institute, suggests that to determine whether an organization is a cult, observe the direction of the power flow. If the power flows from the leadership to the members, it is *not* a cult. However, if the power flows toward the leadership from the followers, it might be.

Dr. Thomas makes the point that adulthood has inappropriately caused the power to flow toward itself. Thus, a cult of adulthood.

Adulthood has both underscored and ballooned its power and influence while stealing influence from both pre-adults and from Elderhood. Thomas suggests the cult of adulthood requires that pre-adults don the mantle of adulthood as soon as possible.

Witness the race to get children and pre-adults into the best schools, illustrated by fierce competition for the best spots as early as kindergarten. This rush conflicts directly with children's need for unstructured time and the power of imaginative play.

Notice also the emphasis on sports in high school, with accompanying competition and huge focus on winning. This has created longer and longer hours of practice which, when added to the demands of homework, leaves little unstructured time to enjoy being a teenager.

At the other end of the scale, adulthood is no longer considered to have an endpoint. Rather, it has taken over the rest of our lifespan as its very own. From the point of view of Adult, it is Adult All The Way. One leaves adulthood only upon death.

How bizarre and rapid this shift has been. Particularly when we consider the 200,000 years during which Elder flourished as our Third Life Stage. Contrast this enormous swath of time with the short 200 years of Elder-loss, a mere *one-tenth of one percent* of humanity's time on Earth.

The Gift from Gaia: Fossil Fuels

From oil and coal have come astounding inventions, from manufacturing to the enormous advances in transportation and communication. Infant mortality has dropped like a stone and our life expectancy has doubled from thirty-five years to seventy-five.

The benefits of these fossil fuels have entered every home and every life – a great gift indeed from our Mother Earth, our beloved Gaia.

Free Energy as a Magic Gift – with Strings Attached

Fossil fuel is a gift with strings.

We are now discovering those strings because they are showing up as thick strands of barbed wire within which we have become entangled, perhaps inextricably so. One wonders whether Elder might have cautioned, "Hey, kids, you Adults, there is no free lunch. Everything has its price and someone, sometime, must pay."

Many Elders did caution, in fact. But where there is no listening, no speaking matters.

Some of the strings include the following:

- String: Free Energy is Running Out
- String: Free Energy Has Byproducts

- String: Global Climate Change
- String: Loss of Connection with self, others and our earth.
- String: Loss of Elder Supervision of Adult
- String: Loss of Family

It Happened Only Two Minutes Ago

The change didn't occur yesterday. It actually occurred *today* when we weren't looking. If we consider the time we humans have inhabited Earth as a single day, the discovery of fossil fuels occurred in the last two minutes.

Humanity had a three-stage life – Youth, Adult, and Elder – for twenty-three hours and fifty-eight minutes. We began to lose our third stage, Elder, *only two minutes ago.*

The Global Fork in the Road

Humanity is now at the most dangerous fork in the evolutionary path since mankind came forth on the planet. Consider the possibility that *had Elder not been lost, humanity might not now be at this fork.*

This is my interpretation. It is an analysis, a story, that I believe will aid us on our path.

The Global Fork

While we have been at forks before, none have been of this magnitude – global. This is the first time in history where our issues have become worldwide rather than regional or national. All regions and nations are now inextricably linked via communication, commerce, travel, and banking.

Fifty years ago, scientists and visionaries alike gave early warnings we were approaching this fork. Elders warned that our addiction to *progress at all costs* was destroying our planet, our home. Adult, embedded deeply in *doing,* deaf and in denial, either ignored or derided those Elders as alarmists.

Upward or Downward?

Some wise thinkers, both scientists and students of possible futures, believe we have gone so far down the path that we are now on the brink of disaster.

Should humanity continue on the downward path, it is possible we shall go over the brink into nightmare.

The Upward Story

On the other hand, there are millions of us all over the world who are on the upward path. We are the ones who believe it is yet possible to turn the world away from the present downward trajectory.

Anyone can easily point to certain facts, some of them critical, which underlie the Upward Story. That you are reading this book is one of those facts, for you are at the tip of a mighty iceberg, a huge group of individuals and organizations dedicated to doing the world good. And there are millions of us.

Note that there are hundreds of books that detail the progress humanity has made, and continues to make, evolving in an upward direction.

There are many facts pointing to humanity's ongoing expansive evolution: increases in measurable well-being, increased life expectancy, decreased infant mortality, more efficient crop production, technological advances, and scores more.

In many ways, these are indeed the best of times. This kind of thinking is expounded on in the books written by Barbara Marx Hubbard who, at eighty-six, has been called by Neale David Walsch, "The greatest living commitment to a world that works for everyone with no one left out."

I am not including a list of the upward or downward trends. I believe part of your job as you train yourself to become an Elder is to research these for yourself. I will, however, emphasize two points of concern.

The Baby Boomer Pig

The Pig in a Python refers to a demographic, the huge population bump called Baby Boomers who are leading the way into Elderhood. There are seventy-five million Americans who were birthed between 1946 and 1964, who are now leaving or about to leave the Adult stage. Our Boomers will either evolve into Elder – or they will … just … get … old.

Facts Underlying the Downward Story

There are many facts underlying the Downward Story. Generally, these fit into four critical areas: Energy, Population, Environment, and Economics. The acronym is EPEE (pronounced *eh'pay*). An epee is a thin light sword that bends easily. This is a useful metaphor because the world's EPEE has been bent to its limits, and some say it is about to snap.

A list of facts underlying the downward trend is included in Appendix 4. You might wish to delay examining these until you have the whole picture I am endeavoring to present. In the meantime, here are two of those facts:

1. It presently takes the resources of almost TWO Earths to support our human population of 7.3 billion.

2. We have ONE Earth.

It is best that you do your own research and come to your own conclusions. You might want to look up Guy McPherson, a man who stares into the abyss. He blogs and uploads lectures to YouTube. Carolyn Baker is a compassionate and knowledgeable historian and social psychologist who blogs and writes books which I find reassuring.

We Live in Angst

According to the *Oxford English Dictionary,* angst is a feeling of deep anxiety or dread, typically unfocused.

Many of us live in a state of angst, carrying a deep sadness in knowing *this is not the way life was intended.* In our dark nights, we are deeply afraid but we don't quite know what we are afraid of. We do not understand why we do not trust.

We do not understand why we don't really know others, and we wonder why we ourselves are not deeply known. We have the sense there is something wrong. There are just too many contradictions.

As Americans, we may realize we live in a world where the most wonderful nation of all, the "beacon on the hill," the cradle of democracy and equality, is also the nation with the world's largest military arsenal. We can look out at a world where forty percent of us live on less than four dollars per day. A world where more than 10,000 babies die *every single day* from malnutrition or malnutrition-related causes.

There Are No Real Shortages

Gandhi said, "There is enough for everyone's need. There is not enough for everyone's greed. There is no shortage of love, though we make it so. There is no shortage of Spirit, except we be blind to it. There is no shortage of compassion and kindness and caring, except as we make it so."

Is There a Way Out?

I find it difficult to see a viable way to shift from our present adolescent worldview of separation. It appears too deeply institutionalized. Our world's institutions – economic, financial, religious, educational, military, and others – seem to be in a perfect correlation with the OR worldview. Change threatens institutions, so they resist it, no matter the cost.

We can only wonder what kind of enormous whack upside the head it might take to transform the institutions, say, of politics or economics from their profound embedment in the OR worldview.

Problems? Or Predicament?

All of the many issues humanity now faces are not separate problems. They are global and they are interlocking.

We might hope that if one problem were solved, others would be as well. I believe this is unlikely. It is questionable that we live within a set of global problems-to-be-resolved. It seems to me we might be living inside a predicament.

Predicaments by their very nature are not solvable – they simply *are.* However, a situation that is a predicament has the possibility of being transformed. A shift from the worldview of OR to a worldview of AND is such a transformation.

To paraphrase Thoreau, "For every thousand working at the problems of the world, there is but one working at the root." And I believe that root to be our present, immature and competitive worldview of OR.

Transformation Is Preceded by Crisis

Transformations do not occur automatically or benignly. Transformation is not mere change. It is an abrupt and sudden shift in state. A transformational shift from OR to AND may not be possible without a major crisis.

There seems to be a fundamental cosmic ground rule that states *Transformation Is Preceded by Crisis.* Evolutionary biologists tell us that this has been true for every evolutionary leap in Earth's five-billion-year past.

We must question, then, whether a worldview transformation from OR to AND can occur without a corresponding crisis. A crisis of this magnitude is almost impossible to comprehend. It is one we just can't wrap our minds around.

Many deeply-spiritual people are asking what we can do (or be), individually or as a group, to make a difference. Perhaps, goes the hope, if I change myself, this will be sufficient. Because as Gandhi said, "Be the change you wish to have happen."

Others live within the grand hope that something will happen in time to help us avoid a crisis of worldwide scope. Perchance an act of God. Or, conceivably, if we were to focus our individual and group attention and energy on a problem we consider to be a core issue, our efforts may result in the other issues dissolving.

Others hope that if we simply ignore the issues they will go away.

This is denial. Seth Godin describes the root of denial on his website which is located at http://sethgodin.typepad.com/sethsblog. He gets it just right:

"Denials all sound the same. They don't come from stupidity. They come from people who won't look. Why [do we] deny? It's a way to avert our eyes.

"Two related reasons, internal and external.

"The external reason is affiliation. What happens

to one's standing when you dare to question the accepted status quo? What are the risks to doing your own research, to putting forth a theory and being prepared to find it proven wrong? What will you tell your neighbors?

"When adherence to the status quo of our faith or organization or social standing looms large, it's often far easier to just look the other way, to feign ignorance or call yourself a skeptic.

"The internal reason is fear. The fear of having to re-sort what we believe. Of feeling far too small in a universe that's just too big.

"Part of being our best selves is having the guts to not avert our eyes, to look closely at what scares us, what disappoints us, what threatens us. By looking closely we have a chance to make change happen."

Denial goes to the core of the problem we now face. Humanity lives in profound denial. We do not know what to do about a predicament, so we do what we usually do. We put the issue aside, focus on the immediate, and live our usual lives – in denial.

This is not an accusation, for denial is not wrong. It is merely human.

Look the Danger Right in the Eye

There are others who choose instead to look the danger directly in the eye. This is Earth after all; we are born here and will each die here. We must ruefully appreciate the joke: "No one gets out of here alive." And, during our precious time on this precarious planet, we know our soft and fragile bodies are always in danger – from water we might drown in, high places we could fall from, sharp things that can wound us.

Because of these and other threats, and because we live with the necessity of food, drink, and weather protection, *there is no real safety.* We cannot live a great life on this planet by striving to be safe. Safety is an illusion.

Yet, the most common question we tend to live inside of, particularly we who live closer to the end of life, is this one: "How can I be most safe?" This is a junior question, for there is no useful answer other than to never arise from bed. And even that is not totally without danger.

A more powerful question is: "How do I live a life of joy, enthusiasm, and compassion *in the face of* the danger that life is?" There is something so freeing and heart-expanding about asking this. It lifts us out of fear and opens the realm of freedom, love, and possibility.

This question is closely akin to another, the ageless question of "What is so?" with its wise answer: "What is so is what is so. And *So what!*" Having asked and replied in this way, we can laugh about this joke. A joke that only the human species can understand.

"So what!" may be the grand joke of the Cosmos.

There IS Something Worth Working On

Once we let that joke settle in, perhaps there *really* is something worth working on. Something worth giving our best to, something so much bigger than ourselves as individuals that it becomes joyous in its hugeness, magnificent in its grandeur.

What if we were to dedicate our lives to bringing back Elder, regardless of how the world turns out? And what if we prepared by exploring the meaning of Elder for ourselves? And training ourselves to become that Elder?

Might this be what we were born to do?

Start by asking yourself the following question: "Does Elder, as a stage of life, and Elderhood as an institution, fulfill a need?" If your answer is yes, then the following questions arise: "What is that need? What was it in the past? What is it now, and what is it likely to be in the future?"

THEN and NOW

Let these questions be present in your mind as I circle back to explore the traditional role of Elder. I want to share with you the role of Elder for the 99.9 percent of the time of our time on this planet. Let's call that vast swath of time – *THEN.* And let's call this evolutionary eye-blink, this one-tenth of one percent of our human history – the last 200 years and 8 generations – *NOW.*

The Role of Elder – THEN

The role of elder to bring wisdom into the world. Elder lived in the family, with the family, and for the family. Youth, Adult, and Elder lived all together within family and within tribe. All learned from each other. Elders were thus trained by five generations – their own generation, plus the pair of generations that preceded them (parents and grandparents), and the pair that followed (children and grandchildren).

The training was built-in and lifelong. It was normal and natural to have five generations of trainers developing the wisdom of an Elder.

Now, it is no longer common for three generations to live under the same roof, particularly in the United States and increasingly in other countries. As a result, our current-day adults arrive at the door of Elderhood trained only by their parents. They arrive semi-trained, if at all.

However, Elder continues on. It still exists, not in the mainstream so much, but in the out-of-the-way places of our world. Elder can be found within indigenous communities, for example, far from the so-called advantages of the modern world. Elder also continues to function within enclaves of immigrants and other groups outside the mainstream of society. Elder continues in the East. And Elder lives on in some Native American cultures.

I posted the following question on Yahoo: *"What is the [present] role of the Elders in Native American Cultures?"*

From a Member of the Suquamish Nation

"In my tribe, the role of the elders is to be a mentor, peacekeeper and storyteller … children and elders have a … deeper understanding of elemental things … they are treated with … respect.

"Children are fresh from another state of being [and] elders are closer to going back to it, so the two bond really well. Kids ask a million and one questions. Elders have a million and one answers, where we adults usually don't have the patience or life experience to answer all of them.

"When a meal begins, elders are served first, with the best cuts of meat and freshest fruit. They have designated seating where they can see/be comfortable while [tribal] work is being done.... Elders are also spoken to with respect and humility....

"The word for 'elder female' is used for all elder females, even one's grandma; there is no distinction. It's the same with 'elder male' (*kiaya* and *tsapa*).

"Elders are consulted if there is a family dispute. The job of the oldest elder in a family is to choose the names of the younger people in the family. I mean our tribal names, not our English ones or nicknames."

Kaha'ka

"In our culture it is the grandparents who teach the children traditions."

Chippewa/Ojibwa

"Elders and children are very important in our society. Although the welfare of children is a common responsibility of the family and community, the responsibility for the welfare of the elders is more pronounced. There is always a place designated for them....

"In community events the elders are always fed first. Special attention is given to elders whether it be in their homes, at public events … in the education system or in community organizations. In every way our elders are consulted as teachers, healers, counselors, in conflict resolution and to pass on our traditional knowledge to the people, especially to the young."

* * * * *

You can read more by doing an Internet search for "the role of elders in indigenous tribes."

Rechee Huff's Story

Rechee Huff, who is African-American and Native American, told me the following story of present-day Eldering:

"During my most challenging period of parenting I am most grateful for my parents' influence on my children. Had I not heeded the lessons learned from my own grandparents and the spiritual guidance about what family really is supposed to be, I do not believe I would have the close relationship with my children I do today.

"When my children were teenagers, I was at a loss how to reach them. I was doing what I thought a parent should do – conversing with them, listening to them, praying with them and for them, vacationing with them, eating as a family, etc. But something was missing and I did not know what. I was at my wit's end. But I was not going to lose them without a fight. I turned to my family for help.

"It began with my sons. They had graduated from high school but were in no hurry to go to college, find a job, or leave the nest. I remembered how things were for me growing up, how I was always sent home for the summer to my grandparents' and the influence that had with me. I called my dad and brothers and asked for help. They consented and I sent my sons to my dad and brother who had a logging business.

"When my sons came back to me in Florida, they obtained jobs and moved into their own apartment together. Today they are married, each with a son of his own. They keep in touch with their grandfather and uncles even today. Later, when my father had an accident in the woods, my sons made it all the way to the country before I did, an 18-hour drive. They did it in 13. They said nothing would keep them from their grandfather.

"Even now when I see either of my sons need a male point of view about something, I suggest they call Dad or one of my brothers.

"My daughter and I could not converse without arguing. The discord was so troubling I called Mom and my sisters. Each called my daughter. We agreed that my daughter should go to one of my sister's homes for a short while.

"Since her return, we have grown closer than ever. Even now, if my mother says anything, it is law for my daughter. She communicates with her grandmother and my sisters regularly. We laugh now about some of those times, although at the time it was not a laughing matter.

"My sisters have had similar experiences. In my turn, I have had visits from my nieces for an intervention. It really is an introduction to life under the guidance of a family member. What they ultimately realize is that as a family we love them and are committed to family.

"It really does take a village to raise a child, as long as it is a balanced village – elders and young ones."

A New Elderhood

Dr. William H. Thomas said the following:

"I believe the elders of our time form the only force capable of returning adult to healthier bounds. So far, this is more hope than reality because relatively few older people have made the leap into elderhood.

"Most choose to live instead as increasingly-enervated adults, marginalized or even exiled from the mainstream of the adult community. Older adults remain, for now, unaware of the nature of elderhood. This is hardly accidental; society explicitly discourages these ideas.

"Still, I am confident that this consciousness will emerge because elderhood has always flourished in affluent societies. It is a hard-bitten tribe that cannot afford to invest in old age.

"By a wonderful coincidence of history, the enlargement of adulthood (which has improved our access to material things) has also created the conditions needed for the emergence of a new elderhood.

"We are stumbling into an era that is blessed with the largest group of (potential) elders the world has ever seen. They are well-educated, materially secure, healthy, and socially engaged. The sad irony is that we live in a time that, like no other before it, has put the treasures of elderhood within the grasp of millions of people."

Elder as Biologic Bedrock

The most basic reason why Elder is critical is anchored in biology. Elder is not just another stage of life. Elder appears to be the *biologic bedrock* of our species.

The stage of Elder may define being human even more than our opposable thumb or our brain's brilliant neocortex.

And Elder itself hinges on an amazing fact – *woman is unique.*

The Surprising Source of Elder: Woman Is Unique

We have completely missed something regarding our own species. This error is a consequence of asking the *wrong* question: "How long can the female of the species closest to humans – chimpanzees – bear young?"

The answer is *for their entire lives.* The human female, however, cannot reproduce all her life. This question produces an uninspiring and wrong-headed answer.

Altering the question produces a powerful answer, one that opens huge possibilities: "What does the female of every mammalian species do when she can no longer produce offspring?"

She dies.

Except for the females of one species. Homo sapiens.

Both questions and answers are based on the same facts. However, the first interpretation, the first story, lives in the realm of limitation. The second story is utterly amazing and unique. It lives in the realm of possibility.

The Human Female Is Unique

When mother can no longer bring us a brother or a sister, she not only does not die, *she remains alive for another half-lifetime.*

Statistics from the National Institute of Aging indicate that the *average* female Baby Boomer was born in 1949, had menopause at age 51 in 2000, and will live until the age of 86. This means she has had an additional 35 years after her childbearing years – to live, love, enjoy, and accomplish. This is more than an additional half a lifetime.

How ironic that our culture has missed something so basic, so in-close. Consider the possibility that our *huge post-reproductive lifespan* may be more important to the success of our species than either our thumbs or our brain size. This interpretation of post-menopausal life opens an enormous possibility.

Perhaps that possibility is for woman to source Elder wisdom. Perhaps the post-reproductive woman is the very source of a new Elderhood.

The Invention of Grandmothers

There is a second irony. Not only have we missed the uniqueness of woman's post-menopausal longevity, we have also missed something else – the incredible importance of grandmothers.

Grandmothers feed and care for their grandchildren. This still occurs today when we show up at Grandma's for the holidays. Yet, such activity was a once-daily event for thousands of generations of families. That is, before the breakdown of family began.

Even now when a baby is born, Grandmother automatically packs a suitcase. Most mothers go help their daughters in a time of newborn overwhelm. When Grandmother arrives, the Three-Generation Unit of Humanity has reunited.

Only Humans Have Grandmothers

Grandmother is an amazing distinction. Evolution invented it. Grandmother *as food provider for grandchildren* does not exist in any other species.

Dr. Thomas observes that this exception points to a rule: All other species of mammals have a two-generational biologic unit – mother and child. In that setup, there is a single generation, mother, to provide sustenance for the child. Human beings, *and human beings alone,* have evolved so that an additional generation, mother's mother, can provide them sustenance. Human babies have an extended dependency that lasts much longer than any other species. This seems to necessitate the three-generational design of Grandmother, Mother, and Child.

Consider the possibility that the evolutionary invention of a caregiving grandmother *may be the very source of Elder.*

The Critical Importance of Old Age

Dr. Thomas writes powerfully of the meaning of old age and of the meaning of grandmothers and grandfathers:

"Old age is our greatest invention.... Old age and the uses to which old age can be put have been shaping our development for hundreds of thousands of years ... we are, as a species, defined by our longevity.

"To grow old is an extraordinary achievement, and around the world and through the ages, people have recognized the value of longevity by creating different social roles for older men and women.

"Menopause, which might seem to be a purely biological phenomenon, also eases the transition to elderhood by ensuring that older women cease ovulating. No longer in direct competition with the younger women around them, they are able to inhabit distinct new social roles.

"Likewise, age whittles male strength and aggressiveness and, with time, ensures the old cannot overthrow the young by force. Secure in this knowledge, adults in traditional societies have long allowed those who reach an advanced age to opt out of the relentless maneuvering for (adult) prestige and power.

"Being freed from the struggle for dominance in the adult hierarchy while still receiving the life-sustaining support and protection of the community is the foundation of our longevity.

"The genius of human aging transforms an inevitable physical decline into something new, a reinvention of the self, a portal that leads to a new freedom from the burdens of adulthood.... Elders have been long granted social shelter in the last decades of life, not as an act of charity, but because old people possess notable talents that make them useful to their families and communities.

"Elderhood came to life when elders became the bearers of human culture. When it comes to retaining, refining, and transmitting culture, elders outperform adults.

"For most of human history ... close daily contact between the young and old was a matter of survival. Being with, watching after, and assisting in the care of young children, while taxing in many ways, does not require the full vigor of youth.

"The physical decline that comes with aging actually cements the relationship between old and young. Indeed, an old man still capable of stalking, killing, and butchering a mastodon would have little inclination to spend hours doting on grandchildren, telling them stories, and instructing them in the ways of their people.

"An old woman still capable of producing young of her own would hardly be inclined to pour time, love, and attention into the lives of her grandchildren. The physiological changes that accompany old age, and upon which contemporary society heaps unlimited scorn, are actually essential preconditions for a socially-productive old age.

"Many other animals employ (and benefit from) a linear transfer of resources from parent to offspring. Humans (by contrast) have evolved a complex, cyclical, three-generation pattern of interdependence. It is this cycle of intergenerational exchange that has propelled the development and ongoing refinement of human language, technology, and culture.

"A child who has been taught and nurtured by his or her elders grows into an adult. An adult equipped with this kind of sophisticated cultural and technical training is well prepared for the work of extracting the necessities of life from an often hostile environment. A rich supple culture helps create the social surplus that is needed if older people are going to be sustained as their vitality wanes.

"When such persons can no longer fulfill the duties of adulthood, they are allowed to put down those burdens and enter into the old age the culture has prepared for them. Safe within its embrace, the elders are free to transmit the fullness of the people's culture to a new generation. The old people tell the stories that the young people use to understand how their lives are to be lived.

"Without old age, Homo sapiens would have been confined to the typical mammalian pattern of a two-generational (childhood and adulthood) social structure. We have used our post-fertility longevity to enlarge the range of human possibility and create a complex web of relationships that brings unprecedented benefits to the community as a whole.

"The social role of *elder of the community* is a brilliant extension of the family-specific role of grandparent. Translating the core elements of grandparenting from the biological to the cultural sphere sparked explosive cultural change. Cross-generational transmission, no longer confined to simple assistance with food and protection, was stretched to include the distinctly human act of communicating meaning.

"There is strong ... support for the idea that human cultures evolve over time and are themselves subject to a form of natural selection. Cultural attributes that provide flexibility and adaptability are likely to succeed and spread. Old age and elderhood have spread from their origin to every point of the globe because societies that embrace and rely on this innovation are more successful than those that do not.

"The discovery of virtue in the necessity of old age is the single greatest achievement in the history of humankind. That we do not understand this as a matter of common sense is a result of the historical glare created by the achievement of adults….

"Old age is far from a forgettable vestige trailing after the bloom of youth. It made our world. It is the greatest of all human creations, the mother of all our inventions."

Ritual Induction

Anthropologists tell us that ritual inductions are worldwide and have existed since man appeared on

Earth. They are the critical doors that delineate the shift from one set of privileges and obligations toward a higher set.

Usually they are created-rituals to powerfully demark stages of life and represent the opening of the gate between Youth and Adult and the gate between Adult and Elder. Ritual inductions correlate both with the physical changes that occur as the individual ages and with the mindset of the new stage.

These inductions have virtually disappeared from so-called civilized societies, remaining as vestigial remnants in some organized religions. Particularly, in the Western culture, there is no longer a ritual induction into the mysteries of Elderhood because there is no Elderhood into which we can be inducted.

My Personal Induction into Elder

In my own case, I was fortunate indeed to be inducted into Elderhood. This occurred prior to leaving my surgical practice.

Anthropologist Rebecca Huss-Ashmore, professor of Anthropology at Penn State, created a ritual for me based on her field experience in Africa, modeling the ceremony after a Maasai ritual. As part of it I was presented with the three symbols of a tribal Elder: a beaded gourd to hold milk, a low three-legged stool upon which I could rest my bony butt (instead of squat-sitting around the campfire as an adult), and a red blanket to warm my shoulders.

I hold all three symbols dear.

BOOK TWO

THE ELDER TRAINING

"Nothing is so powerful as an idea whose time has come." – Victor Hugo (The Hunger Project)

The Necessity of Elder

Elder is needed. This is my belief, and this is the reason for this book.

The Path to Elder is *unrelated* to the question of which road humanity will take, upward or downward. Taking the Elder Path is a function of your inner world, not a function of what is occurring in the outer world. The life and experience and joy of being an Elder are independent of circumstance.

Choosing the Elder Path is a matter of its own.

Be Aware of Both Roads

Yet, it is good to be aware of both roads and remain conscious of your conclusions about each. If you conclude we might turn the world around in time, then the following quote from Margaret Mead may inspire you:

> *"Never doubt that a small group of committed individuals can change the world. In fact it is the only thing that ever has."*

Should a crisis not occur for a long time to come, then becoming an Elder might be critical in transforming the OR paradigm without crisis.

On the other hand, you may believe "The Crunch" or "The Long Emergency," a vast crisis by whatever NAME, will occur, perhaps soon. If you do, then the compassion of Elder will be necessary so you may support our brothers and sisters and children as we face whatever comes. Should the very worst happen, perhaps those who become Elder on this planet will have a role elsewhere/elsewhen. We might then become privy to the long view that humanity was once a Grand Idea in the Mind of God – amazing while it lasted.

There are, of course, many intermediate possibilities. One is that humanity will survive in isolated pockets and a new set of indigenous cultures will arise, cultures founded on the AND worldview. Elder can serve to ensure that the detour into our present OR worldview will be the road *not* taken.

> *"Although an infant becomes a child simply by aging, a person cannot become an elder by simply becoming older. Elders fall into the category of things that are made, not born.*
>
> *"Becoming an elder is not a 'natural occurrence'; the qualities needed don't simply develop from physical changes brought on by aging. Rather, there is something metaphysical involved; something philosophical and spiritual required. Old age alone doesn't make the elder."*
>
> – Michael Meade, *Fate & Destiny: The Two Agreements of the Soul*

The Time to Train (to Relearn) Is Now

Clearly, it would have been better if Elder had been reestablished earlier. And it would have been best if Elder had not been lost in the first place. Yet, there is no blame. The Loss of Elder is one of the correlates of the thinking that humanity has done to date.

Elder loss is simply one aspect of the Great Package of Our Times.

A Pair of Tasks

It seems that Adults are being asked at this global fork in the road to perform a pair of tasks:

1. To train ourselves (relearn) to become Elders; and

2. To teach others to become Elders.

These two tasks are embedded in the heart of family; these tasks are embedded IN the heart of tribe. They reside also at the heart of co-creating humanity's future with each other and with Spirit. Perhaps you will choose to place them in your own heart.

A great future for humanity without Elder is an oxymoron. Without a return to a Three Stage Life, we will become just another mammalian species like the chimpanzee. This would not constitute evolution … rather, a devolution.

There Is No Prescription for How to Grow Old

Everyone grows old, of course. And we all do it differently.

How we grow old depends on many factors: how others in your family grew old, what your expectations are, your ideas about health and education and illness, and your background commitment to live long or not. How you grow old is also dependent on your emotions, whether you tend to be joyous or depressed, enthusiastic or resigned, angry or happy, expectant or cynical.

There is no prescription for how to grow old.

There IS a Prescription for Elderhood

Becoming an Elder is different. There is a prescription for Elderhood. However, our culture has dis-remembered most of what that entails, just as we have dis-remembered the role of family, village, traditions, and the communication between generations.

This second half of the book is about re-examining that prescription, that path. It can serve as a blueprint to train yourself to become an Elder.

Be Easy About This

There is no obligation to take action. Elder may be required, but you, as an individual, are *not* obliged to take the Elder Path. Perhaps you believe your contribution is in the past and you have "done your stint." I have no issue with this, nor should anyone else, especially not you. This is, after all, your own precious life to live. You will live it your way.

However, for those who might think their life is over, or who believe they missed the opportunity to make a contribution, I say this: You might be mistaken. If you are still alive, it is simply too soon to say. Your biggest contribution might still be ahead.

For example, you might one day speak of or do that *one particular thing.* And it might just alter another person's life completely. Yet you may never discover that you made such an impact. In the words of master salesman Zig Ziglar, "You never know when a moment and a few sincere words can have an impact on a life."

Emphasis is on the *"You never know."*

Do know this: You do NOT need to embark on the specific Elder training that follows. You can simply listen to others, be compassionate with them, and perhaps speak a few sincere words. In doing so, you will have taken an action right in front of you. And perhaps have made an impact.

Further, you can honor yourself as Elder – with or without Elder training.

The Elder Journey: General Introduction

"Elder is the Lost Gift of Life." – Arleen Bump

"Elder is the essential aspect of our survival." – P.E. Collins

Clearly, the journey goes from Adult to Elder. Generally, the path is from later Adult to Elder, although sometimes young people find themselves on an Elder journey.

The journey is not straight because growth does not work that way. Personal growth occurs as leaps, with periods of quiescence. This quiescence is more apparent than real, for it is a time of assimilation of what has been learned during the leap.

Furthermore, the path is more circuitous than straight. The path often appears to double back on itself, perhaps to pick up something not quite assimilated.

A useful metaphor for the Elder Path is the onion. As an onion grows, it expands from the center to form rings. But, unlike the onion, the leap of layers for a human does not have an endpoint. The expansive leaps come faster and higher and the growth of wisdom becomes exponential.

Re-invention of the Distinctions

As a result of our eight-generational detour, our devolutionary down-step, *we must re-invent the important distinctions within Elder Training.* What was once implicit must be made explicit.

This book is not intended to be definitive. Rather it is a first cut at this critical topic. Other writers can be expected to amplify or alter my views.

I recommend that you do not consider this material as merely a book to be read once and set aside. While it is fine to read it through to get the whole picture, I suggest that you hold it as a *training manual* to be read repeatedly as you self-train as an Elder. You will be wiser each time you return and you will see what you did not see before. Think of it as your companion as you grow in Elderhood.

Basic Steps to Train Yourself As Elder

1. Intend to do so. This spoken and internal intention puts you on the path.

2. Intend for guidance to show up.

3. Say YES to what shows up, particularly something outside your comfort zone. Be open.

4. Be vulnerable. Let your guard down and allow yourself to feel hurt. Be willing to share from the heart.

5. Begin to meditate. Meditation quiets the mind.

6. Seek out others on the path and dialogue with them.

7. Join a group of seekers. Do not concern yourself too much with what they seek. It is their *seekerness* you need to associate with.

8. Restore your integrity.

9. Complete your past.

10. Practice forgiveness. Forgive anything and everything you perceive was done to you. Include forgiving yourself.

11. Surrender to not knowing. Question everything you believe. Be willing to be shaken and confused. Confusion is a high space.

12. Trust the process. Allow Spirit to work through you.

13. Listen/Trust/Speak. Repeat.

To take on any of these is to *be on the path.* When on the path, there is no particular sequence. Any circumstance, any thought, any upset, can serve as *Grist for the Mill,* as Ram Dass titled one of his books.

Do not look all the way down the path; take one step after another. If you veer off the path by mistake, don't worry. You will automatically return to the path and discover it was not a mistake after all. Rather, the veering was required.

There Is No Right Path

There is a part of us, the Adult-thinking part, which looks for the *right path.* There is no right path.

Notice when you find yourself thinking you are doing the path *right* or doing it *wrong.* This is inaccurate. So smile kindly on yourself.

Also, there is no *better* path. Your path is your path. It is uniquely yours, though not as unique as your mind might think. The right path, whether clear to you now or not, is *the path you took.* Only by looking back will you see the truth of that.

Looking forward, trust. Here's a saying I learned to trust, as suggested by Carole Kammen, founder of Temenos and Pathways: "Something there is that leads my life and it looks not like me."

What follows are some guidelines. There is only one rule on the path: trust yourself. This is your time. Throw a vision into the future of becoming wise. Then trust this future vision to pull you into itself.

Cultural Undergrounds

All cultures have undergrounds, pockets consisting of quiet or even secret groups. There have always been gatherings of the wiser among us who are aware there is something *off* about the culture.

At the height of the patriarchy, when women had no voting rights, no economic rights, when they were beaten, sidelined, and disparaged, women formed underground groups. Women talked together. They kept a spirit alive amongst themselves. They did this in secret, keeping guard against being overheard.

Their groups were conspiracies to survive and to do *good* in the world. There was Goodness in them, there was danger in them, and there was Godness in them.

These same kinds of undergrounds exist in all cultures hostile to the full expression of the human spirit. They existed in the killing times of Hitler, in the times of the early Christians and during the Diaspora of the Jews. And they existed during the time of American slavery and through the subsequent era of immense segregation.

We can easily imagine that they have existed among all of the slave communities of the twenty-one previous major civilizations on our planet.

More broadly, there is an underground wherever there is suppression of the human spirit – in places of worship and in kitchens, in basements and in tents.

In present times, there are quiet organizations of Elders. They consist mostly in indigenous tribes, but they also exist in cities and suburbs. Many are in the process of organizing themselves. Some have websites and are on the Internet, waiting for you to join them. They are waiting for you to share with them, endorse them, walk with them, train with them. And perhaps to lead them.

These underground organizations are the outward manifestation of a profound conversation. The Underground Conversation.

The Underground Conversation

The Underground Conversation of the Human Spirit is always present within every culture. This underground conversation lies beneath both the foreground and the background conversations. This conversation is the Good-within speaking, the God-within.

To distinguish the three layers of the conversation of a culture, use the Three Face metaphor. As individuals, we each have an *outer* smiling face we show to the world. This mask covers the frowning, self-centered, and survival-oriented *inner* face, the face we hide.

Beneath both masks there is our *true* face, the radiant face of our essence, our true self. The true face is the face of love, giving, compassion, and forgiveness. It is where *The Bond* lives, so eloquently described by Lynne McTaggert in her book of the same name.

Just as we have our true face, so too do we have our true conversation. This is the conversation of our soul, of our Essence. I call this the Underground Conversation.

The bottom line of this conversation is a commitment to *a world that works for everyone with no one and nothing left out.* This was first expressed by Werner Erhard in the 70s and is equally valid today.

This notion can also be expressed as the worldview of AND. The Underground Conversation within each of us has manifested in the world as a particular group of organizations.

Mystery Schools

For millennia, quiet organizations known as Mystery Schools have been in existence, their purpose being to keep critical knowledge and understanding alive during times of great stress in the world. Mystery Schools have long served humanity by being a solid and secret bridge spanning from one time of human freedom to another across the dangerous chasm of wars, pestilence, and dictatorships.

Mystery schools have served as guardians of freedom and the expansion of the human spirit. Through a fraternity or sorority of committed men and women, the mission and purpose has been to study the secrets of Humanity and the Universe. They keep the Underground Conversation alive.

Examples include the ancient Druidic and Eleusinian Mystery Schools, Alchemy, Kabbalah and Freemasonry. There are also modern mystery schools. I was a member of the Pathways Institute Mystery School for several years.

Seymour Conspiracies

Most benevolent organizations, however, are less formal, and often have a more local vision. These organizations have been designed to do good in the world. I call all of them *Seymour Conspiracies.*

This metaphor originates from a story by J.D. Salinger. In *A Perfect Day for Banana Fish,* Seymour Glass is a shell-shocked Korean War veteran. He thinks the world is conspiring, a common enough delusion in the paranoid. Seymour, however, is convinced the world is conspiring to do him *good.* "I am a kind of paranoiac in reverse. I suspect people of plotting to make me happy."

Seymour Conspiracies consist of gatherings of good people conspiring to benefit the world. These can be training grounds for Elders. Sometimes they are international organizations such as the Red Cross, Search for Common Ground, The Hunger Project, and Amnesty International. Sometimes they are national, like Boy Scouts and Girl Scouts, Results, and Kiwanis Club of America.

These organizations, referred to as NGOs, or Non-Governmental Organizations, exist in wild profusion. The number of NGOs operating in the United States is estimated at one and a half million.

Russia is reported to have 277,000 NGOs, and India has more than 2 million.

Where to Start

If you look at the list of the many courses, retreats, and seminars I have taken (Appendix 2) and pointed randomly to one, stating, "I will start here," this would probably be a good place to start. All chosen paths lead to Elder. A wisdom education is a transformational education is an Elder Training.

However, there is only one program on the list that, in my personal experience, has the depth, breadth, and longevity to be called a Wisdom Education. Landmark Worldwide's *Curriculum For Living* begins with the powerful three-day experience of The Landmark Forum. If all those taking their courses, now presented in 115 cities worldwide, were gathered in one place, it would be the largest university in the world.

Landmark does not advertise, relying instead on word of mouth. You do not hear about it by accident, but deliberately. You are told about it by a graduate who sees something special in you. Landmark's personal development and leadership work is not for everyone. It is for those who are *up to something.* As you are.

Compilation of Wisdom

Much of what follows is a compilation of the wisdom I have gained from three sources: first, from the learnings gained from my forty-five-year surgical career; second, from the courses I have taken from Landmark Worldwide; third, from the profound influence of my participation in more than twenty-five courses in other disciplines, most of which were spiritually based. My take on these teaching and learnings, however, is my own.

The Necessity of Experiential Work

What I share in this book can only serve as background and will not be a substitute for experience. My learnings came from trainings, and these trainings are all experiential. Simply reading the material presented here is like reading a book titled *How to Ride a Bicycle.* You do not learn to ride a bicycle from reading a book. You learn to ride a bicycle by riding a bicycle.

I am not disparaging the value of reading. When one is open, material comes from everywhere and anywhere. Read it all. You can open books at random or throw a dart at a reading list and read whichever book gets pierced. There is more to a guided dart than meets the eye.

So my advice is to immerse yourself in reading. But not to the exclusion of experiential work.

Vulnerability

There are attributes of Elderhood that either do not exist in Adulthood or are so neglected or disparaged that they have become rudimentary. One example is vulnerability.

The aphorism *Zen mind, beginner's mind* is apropos because it can also mean *Elder mind, child mind.* This concept entreats us to be as a child and open to possibility. It entreats us to trust others enough to be vulnerable with them, deliberately lowering our shield against hurt. It entreats us to trust our own inner knowing that we *cannot* be hurt by others. We are being asked to open ourselves to others in spite of our fear that we *can* be hurt.

To be an Elder means to be vulnerable, to be open to what others have to say. To be vulnerable despite the fear of being hurt. "Vulnerability is not weakness," says Brene Brown, researcher, "It is courage. Vulnerability is also the birthplace of creativity and innovation and adaptability to change."

She gives a TED Talk, "The Power of Vulnerability." She really nails it. I cried when I watched it, as, I believe, will you. You can watch it by going to the following link:

http://www.youtube.com/watch?v=iCvmsMzlF7o

or by searching "TED … Brene Brown … vulnerability."

To be an Elder also means to be open to possibility. Possibility is not in the same realm as *probability* or *likelihood*. Rather, possibility exists in a realm of its own, along with openness, creativity, imagination, and a wide open future.

Possibility offers an open method of thinking that is the opposite of thinking-as-usual. Such openness is akin to living within a world of *Yes!* in contrast to living within a world of *No!*

So, consider the possibility of living in possibility.

The Elder Journey: Specific Introduction

Why would *you* train yourself to become an Elder instead of just getting old?

In the first place, becoming an Elder is inherent to being human. Second, you really have nothing better to do. Third, if you have read this far, you are already on the path. And fourth, it is the only worthwhile way to grow old. Plus, you do love a challenge, don't you?

The greatest possible context for Elder seems to be this: Elder is the Last, for which the First was made. Elder is the culmination of Youth's grandest aspiration. Elder is what is inside Youth, in the same way that the acorn contains the oak tree. Elder is what always was, is now, and shall forever be. Elder is what you chose to be born to become. Elder is the Essence of Being Human – a Humane Becoming. Elder is the personification of Spirit-in-Action.

What is often forgotten is that Elder is not only wise, but playful. An essential aspect of being an Elder is play. The struggle has stopped, the resistance has ended, and things have gotten easier. Elders love to play. There is the fun, the joy, and the excitement of interactions, whether in a game, a joke, or a conversation.

Life is so much easier in the Elder stage.

Parable: The Joke at the Return Party

When you pass over, you find yourself at a gathering of all those who passed before you and have come to welcome you back. Amidst the hugs and joviality, you get the sense there is a joke and everyone is in on it except you.

Finally, you understand that you are the butt of the joke. And the joke is this: "It didn't *have* to be that hard, you know!" Your mouth hangs open for a moment before you laugh, realizing they are right. It did *not* have to be that hard.

Consider the possibility that you did not show up here, on Earth at the most dangerous and most critical time in the history of humanity by accident. You demanded to ride this rollercoaster. You chose to both witness and participate in this time of mankind's greatest challenge. You chose to be born right around NOW.

So, welcome! I may be a bit late in my welcome, but it is heartfelt.

Now, in your mid- or late-Adult stage, just when you imagined you would sit back and take it easy, resting in your armchair and watching TV, along comes this opportunity to take the Elder Path.

However, this is not the Path-to-Elder of the long-distant past in which you were trained over many decades by your family's five generations.

That was THEN and this is NOW. That was a natural path and this one is not. This one will be a much more demanding mistress, for the time to train yourself is short and our planet seems to be hanging in the balance and in need of your service.

Your Personal Fork in the Path

So you find yourself here at your own personal fork. One path, the one *most* traveled, is the path taken by default; that is, you just get old. This is the easy, comfortable, and familiar path that leads inexorably to the waiting room of the funeral parlor.

The other path is hidden behind the bushes with a beaten-up sign reading, *Elder-in-Training*. This path was once paved with gold, but it is now covered with dead leaves, disheveled with weeds, and there are tree branches snapping in your face.

So you are being invited, or you are inviting yourself, to take this path less traveled. It is the path that will assault your mountain of Ego, pass you through the Slough of Despair, and mire you in the Swamp of the Past. And you will have to pass through the barbed wire fields of our Cynical Culture of Ageism.

At the same time, it is the path of joy, the path of satisfaction, the path of Good. This is the path of enthusiasm for your magnificent life. The path of outward-looking and discovering.

It is the path of giving. It is the extraordinary path taken by ordinary people. It shines brightly, in sharp contrast to the usual path of looking for what you can *get* out of life.

It is also the path of the co-creation of humanity's future – with others, and with Spirit.

Fellowship

The Elder Path is a solitary path, and yet it is not. You will find many on the same journey. You will meet them as though long-lost friends, and you will embrace them with familiarity as family. You will discover you have found a home. The Elder Journey is the Big Time.

And what is at the other end of this path? There is no other end. It is not about the destination, you see, it is about the journey itself. There is no top to the mountain and you will never become a finished Elder. You will always remain, through the last hours and minutes of your dying, an *Elder-in-training.*

Bad news? No, good news. Knowing this will keep you humble. And humility is one of the attributes of Elder.

The Easy Path

I recently had an epiphany. I had long wondered about the popularity of adult communities like The Villages in Florida with its population of 51,000, ninety-five percent over the age of sixty. Upon visiting briefly, it had felt so, well, contrived.

Recently, I attended an intimate concert where I observed the interaction between violin magician

Valenti Imerelli and virtuoso pianist Brian Murphy. I was struck by how these musicians riffed off each other, how expressive their faces and bodies became as they danced their music back and forth, each watching the other's expression. It was a musical conversation of joy, humor, and delight.

I realized that, to them, this was *play.* They were *playing.* Musically. Oh. So that's what is meant by *playing music.*

When I expressed this to Murphy, he nodded vigorously and quoted George Bernard Shaw, "You don't stop playing when you grow old. You get old when you stop playing." Yes, exactly.

And that's when I understood The Villages and what they might represent to many older people. In a world that no longer appreciates Elders, either as wisdom-carriers or as contributing humans, The Village and places like it are a great place to live. Why hang around where we are not wanted? Why not go to where we are appreciated?

And who is easier to hang out with than our peers than in a summer camp for Adults, a Disneyland for the disenfranchised? Where better to have playmates and live a life of play?

As we enter into our last third of life, we have a choice. As Elders, we can create a life of contribution and compassion and play right where we are. Or we can say the hell with it and go where life is already comfortably laid out for us, full of exciting activities and conversation with others like ourselves.

Did I make that option sound attractive? I meant to.

Which will you choose? There is no obligation to finish this book. No obligation to train yourself as Elder. Pure choice.

Personally, I am staying on the Elder Path. Mainly because it seems to me this is why I was born at this time. Care to join me?

Having said all that, having set up an either/or situation, it is *not* a matter of choosing one or the other. The Elder Path is a joyous path, a playful path and you can live in the midst of great fun during your Elder-in-training. After all, there is need for Elders wherever there are people, no matter if they are all adults.

Step One

If you choose to take the Elder Path, the first step is to declare yourself an Elder. Do this now. No kidding.

Remember, Elder is a stage, not an age. Your chronological age is irrelevant. Nor should you ask yourself whether you are ready. If you have read this far, you are old enough and ready enough. You may trust me on this.

Go stand in front of a mirror. Look that person in the eye and pause until the mind's conversation has settled. Then make the declaration: *I hereby declare I AM AN ELDER.*

Do not read further until you have completed this task. You must actively take this stand. It will set the tone for everything that follows.

Elder Training is not a passive activity; it is participatory. Everything must be done by playing on the court rather than by observing from the stands. This is not a casual book to provide information. It is not a book as much for the *interested* as it is for the *committed.* It is a guide to Transformation. And Transformation takes work.

So go to the mirror right now. Take step number one. Make your declaration. With this declaration, you create and endorse yourself.

No declaration: No Elder.

Say YES to What Is in Front of You

When the pupil is ready the teacher will arrive. Sometimes the teacher is a human being, sometimes a course, sometimes a book or a pamphlet. Note that you are reading *this* book. A teacher, perhaps? You may discover there are no coincidences in life. Be ready because the universe will throw stuff at you. The universe loves Elder.

For instance, you might start to notice advertisements for courses you had not noticed before. You might spot a sign you'd never noticed before. One that says, "Psychic. Come in."

Well, don't just stand there, go on in.

A friend might tell you about The Landmark Forum. You might overhear a conversation about a speaker coming to town. Because you are open your opening will get filled. Trust it.

Reconsider yourself as one who says YES to whatever you are asked or invited to do. Lead your life as if *something is leading your life and it looks not like you.*

Two Kinds of Education

To fully grasp the depth and breadth of the Elder Training, we must examine our ideas and assumptions about education. Our culture's ideas about education are in the way of the Elder Training. Education as we have understood it blocks the path to achieving wisdom, to becoming an Elder.

There are two distinct kinds of education, although we are trained to think there is only one. Our thinking-as-usual has missed something crucial.

***In*formational Education**

I benefitted from thirteen years of formal education following high school – college, medical school, and surgical residency. Mine was, in retrospect, an amazing and wonderful education for which I am everlastingly grateful.

The information I learned in college created a foundation for understanding science – chemistry, physics, zoology and comparative anatomy. These subjects were in addition to the broader courses I took in English, history, sociology, and psychology.

In medical school, I learned information I needed to function as a physician – human anatomy, biochemistry, physiology, bacteriology, psychiatry, and others. In my general surgical training, I spent three years within all of the various surgical subspecialties to become conversant with terminology and procedures. This meant general surgical surgery itself, plus thoracic surgery, gynecology, neurosurgery, urologic surgery, and more.

During my plastic surgical training, I learned to understand, assist and perform all the surgical procedures of this specialty, including the care of massive burns, the treatment of congenital deformities, the treatment of cancer of the head and neck, the surgical repair of trauma.

These treatments were in addition to training in the surgery of improved appearance – cosmetic surgery.

Thus my formal education, my *in*formational education, consisted of the acquisition of multiple bodies of knowledge.

Then I did the *est* training, and something in me opened up. I received the first certainty that I was, finally, on the right track. The *est* training *opened a depth of knowing I had been unaware even existed.*

Additional courses and seminars, such as the Hoffman Quadrinity Process and workshops with Elisabeth Kübler-Ross, Neale Donald Walsch, and Don Miguel Ruiz, added the emotional and spiritual realms to what had been almost exclusively an *intellectual* education.

These courses opened insights into being more fully human and offered new perspectives so I could experience life more fully. I became a searcher, seeking out course after course (see Appendix 2).

I am no longer a seeker, yet I continue to be a student.

*Trans*formational Education

The new education I received in those courses revealed to me that there are, at the core, two quite different educational systems. I had previously believed there was only one, the one we in the West simply refer to as *education.*

The two types of education are *in*formational and *trans*formational. Both are distinct. They exist in different realms. This is important for an Elder-in-training to realize because *trans*formational education provides insights from which arise wisdom in general and the wisdom of the Elder in particular.

Furthermore, gaining a *trans*formational education is the essential difference between becoming an Elder and being someone who just gets old.

To distinguish these two realms of education, I will, with their permission, utilize the diagram Landmark Worldwide uses to introduce their work:

The Two Realms of Education

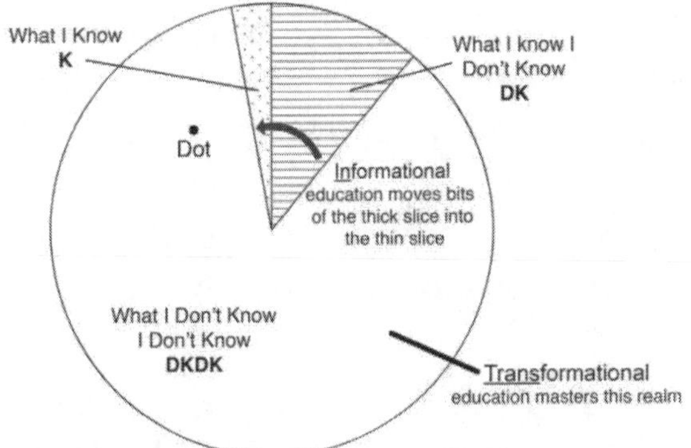

The Circle represents everything that can be known. A tiny dot represents what any one person knows. To be generous, the thin slice represents this.

The larger slice represents what we know we don't know.

The enormous remainder is the realm of the DKDK, where resides everything we Don't even Know we Don't know.

Diagram #1: © Landmark Worldwide

Let us represent everything that can possibly be known by a circle. We can represent what a single person knows by a tiny dot. To be generous, let us use a thin slice, rather than a dot, to represent What I Know (K). We know our name, how to read, the distinctions of our careers, etc. For instance, I know how to perform surgery, how to tie fishing flies, and how to drive home.

A larger slice represents what I Don't Know (DK). I know, for instance, that I do not know ancient Swedish, how to fly a plane, and what the other side of the moon looks like.

The remainder of the circle is the realm of what I Don't even Know I Don't Know (DKDK).

More on *In*formational Education

The primary purpose of an informational education seems to be the transfer of information from the slice, What I Don't Know, to the smaller slice called, What I Know. This is a great purpose indeed. Yet most people assume this to be the total purpose of education, particularly those in the United States.

We inherited this purpose from John Dewey, the powerful educator who, in 1934, declared it was "to give the young the things they need in order to develop in an orderly, sequential way into members of society."

A useful purpose for cogs in a machine; not so great a purpose for humans of infinite variety and potential.

More recently, the purpose of education has shifted. Here is a description from 1991: "The one continuing purpose of education, since ancient times, has been to bring people to as full a realization as possible of what it is to be a human being."

Having taken both educational paths, I have become convinced most that this "full realization" resides within the DKDK realm. We are not giving students what they need to lead a full life, a life of openness, freedom and possibility.

Transformational education provides insights into being human. This kind of education opens up the deeper experiences of life and allows us to experience life from new perspectives.

Such learning goes right to the core of being human. It is the realm where our blind spots reside. A blind spot is an unconscious and erroneous belief akin to thinking we can steer our car by adjusting the rearview mirror. Bad beliefs can have bad effects. We may be blind to our personal blind spots, but our friends are less likely to be.

Personal Blind Spots

When I was young, I assumed socks were like shoes and had lefts and rights. It took me a while to dress because I couldn't decide which sock was which. My blind spot, of course, was I was not aware a sock fits either foot.

Another personal blind spot occurred when I was a little older. At the time, I was unaware how much I interrupted conversations. Then my mother began counting my interruptions out loud. I was shocked how quickly the numbers mounted. Another blind spot.

Transformational work reveals that some of our individual blind spots are immense and interfere with living with grace and ease. Small blind spots can cause big problems.

Cultural Blind Spots

Most importantly, most of our blind spots are *cultural,* generally unavailable to us. There are even *humanity-wide* blind spots that exist outside our worldview. I will say more about these later.

Cultural blind spots contain the assumptions we have about ourselves (Who, what, and where are we?), the assumptions we have about others (Are we connected or separate?), and about how the cosmos works (Is the universe kindly, indifferent or hostile? Is there Spirit?).

These questions remain unconsciously unasked in our day-to-day lives, yet we live inside the automatic and unconscious answers. These unconscious answers set the tone, purpose, and direction of our lives.

What Else Resides in the DKDK Realm?

Everything we are blind to lives in the DKDK realm. Here reside the nested contexts of our lives. Creativity has its palace here. Imagination builds its castles here too. In addition, the DKDK realm includes all we *believe* to be true but often is not true at all.

Consider that the study of this realm constitutes a wisdom education. We can also consider it to be the realm of ontology, *the study of being.* Cosmology is the study of the being-ness of human beings. It is the study of the commonality, the sameness, of every single one of us humans.

The Clear and Obvious Value of Our *In*formational Education

Our *in*formational education system has proven incredibly useful, particularly when mounds of data, facts, and information must be learned. It has produced, as an obvious example, our worldwide communication system and other spectacular advances in technology.

What Distinguishes Them

*Trans*formational education is about noticing, examining and choosing *contexts,* whereas *in*formational education confines itself to *content* accumulation, focusing little, if at all, on the context within which information is held.

*Trans*formational education occurs best in a group setting. Group learning is a very different experience, akin to the joy of group singing in contrast to singing by yourself in your living room. It is a more powerful experience by far. By contrast, aloneness works perfectly well in acquiring an *in*formational education.

Results Distinguish the Two

Most importantly, these two educational realms are distinguished by their results. The results produced via an *in*formational education are incremental and additive.

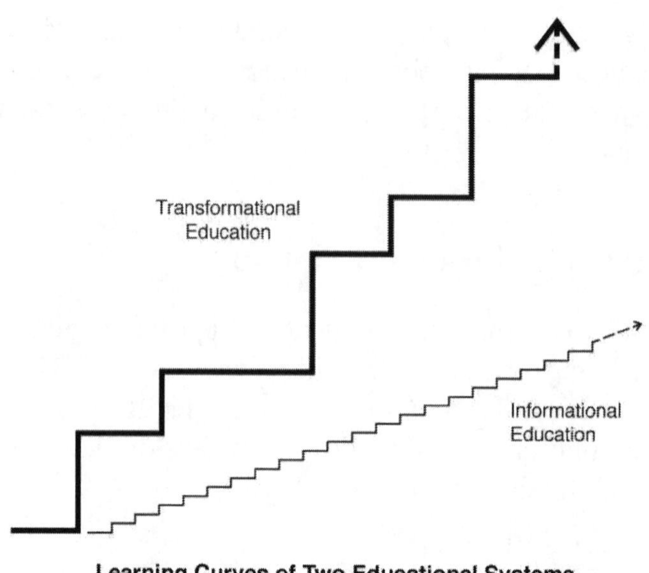

Learning Curves of Two Educational Systems

Diagram #2

Walking up the stairs of an *in*formational system, there are many small steps to climb and with each we reach a small new level. In the case of our usual education, results tend to occur slowly, over the course of years. In my case, there were twenty-five years of *in*formational education before I was qualified to enter surgical practice.

Think of *trans*formational education as akin to the sudden appearance of an elevator that can jump-lift you to the penthouse. *Trans*formational education produces results as sudden leaps of insight, leading to profound understanding. Such insights can reorient all past knowledge.

For instance, at a course I was taking one student shared his sudden insight that his life-long attitude of "you owe me" had poisoned his relationships within his family, particularly with his mother. This epiphany altered the way he had viewed his mother.

"I suddenly realized she had birthed me and raised me and *she owed me nothing!* Instead, I was clear that hers was a gift of her love for me. My insight was so sudden it felt like it occurred outside of time."

Another student in a course I took spoke of the experience of his results as "occurring exponenttially."

Extraordinary Results

I have been present during such revelations many times, both within my own thinking and feeling as well as in the experiences of hundreds of others. The transformation is visible. Faces soften, postures straighten, and bodies loosen. Anger disappears, resentments vanish, and fears dissipate. Smiling happens. Laughter happens.

Barriers to living powerfully and joyfully simply fade away. These are replaced by courage and a fearlessness that is true freedom. Participants speak of a new enthusiasm and joy. There is frequently a background shift from a need to *get* to a desire to *give.*

Someone once told me that this sounded too good to be true. I had to agree that yes, after a solid background in our usual kind of education, such a statement does indeed sound that way. But the results are the results.

The Ladder of Holarchy

We can use another metaphor to help distinguish *trans*formational education. Imagine a ladder representing the acquisition of knowledge. This ladder is unusual because each rung contains everything in the rungs below. Such inclusion means the ladder represents a *holarchy* rather than a *hierarchy.*

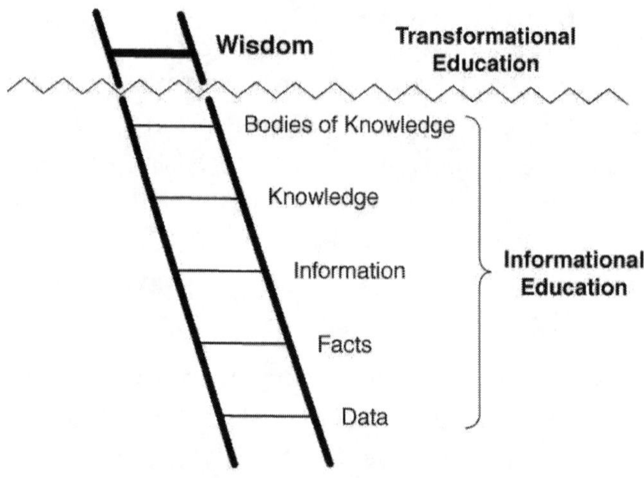

The Ladder of the Holarchy of Knowledge

Diagram #3

Starting at the bottom, label each ascending rung as *Data, Facts, Information, Knowledge,* and *Bodies of Knowledge.* At the *Bodies of Knowledge* rung, *in*formational education stops. The rung above is missing. We might speak of the missing rung as *the appropriate application of bodies of knowledge for the well-being of all Earth's creatures.* I might also call it the *Wisdom* rung or the rung of the *Wise Elder.*

This is the realm of *trans*formational education, the realm of DKDK.

Distinct but Inseparable

Now that we have distinguished them, it is important to realize both educational types go together and overlap. Each is distinct but inseparable. As a simple example of "distinct but inseparable," the terms *body* and *chest* are each a useful distinction. They also *go together.* Thus, we can speak of them as *distinct but inseparable.*

Of great import to the success of Elder Training is the realization that Elder *as a distinction* resides in the vast and fascinating realm of DKDK.

Basic Paradox of Life

A Hindu proverb states, "There are three things that cannot be known: Air to the bird, water to the fish, and mankind to himself." Yet the instruction to humankind from time immemorial has been "Know Thyself!"

The paradox is expressed by the question, "How might we know that which cannot be known?"

The answer is, "By waking up!"

This answer lies within the realm of DKDK, the realm of transformational education.

Summary

The outcome of a transformational education is the kind of magnificent and adventurous life each of us came here to live. As Helen Keller once said, "Life is either a daring adventure, or nothing." We can each choose, at any age, to live a life of grand adventure. Or we can live an ordinary life and just … get … older.

A transformational education consists of straightforward exercises and practices resulting in insights which, in turn, remove the barriers to living an extraordinary life. This can lead to a life of freedom, possibility, and workability – our birthright.

Clear Out the Clutter

One of the major challenges of becoming an elder is to create a clear space so that a powerful future is possible. We do not leave the world of Adult and enter the world of Elder with a clear space. Rather, we enter with a space full of our past.

Our past is full of opinions, judgments, assumptions, standards, and memories of hurts and injustices. And it is full of righteousness. Our *present* is so hooked by the past that it boxes us into a prison. That unseen box lives within the DKDK realm. Only by clearing out the past can we have a clear space. And only in this clear space can we create a future that is other than the past.

To accomplish this, the clutter of the past must be cleared out. Then the past can be put back where it belongs – in the past. Vulnerability is the key to the clearing out. And the keys to vulnerability are truth-telling and responsibility.

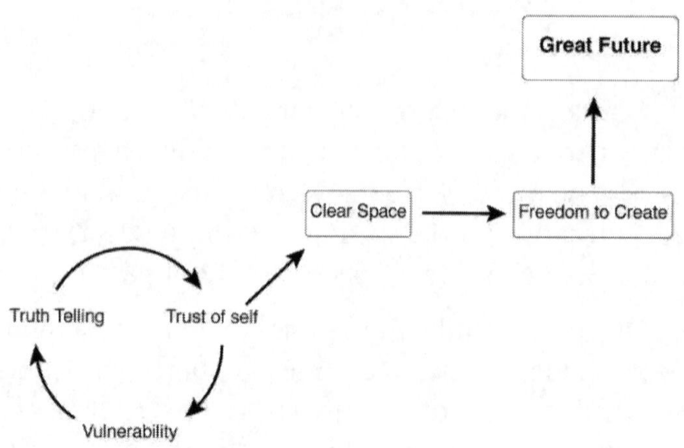

Completing Your Past – The way it works.

Diagram #4

How Human Beings Work: Mind and Self

A powerful model will help us to understand how human beings work, both you and others.

Ontology

There is a commonality to how every single human being works. We are not speaking of our obvious differences, the study of which is called psychology. Rather, we are interested in the *sameness* of every one of us. As I wrote earlier, ontology examines this question: "What is the nature of the *being* of all human beings?"

A Model of How Humans Work

This particular model asks you to consider that there are two of you – the Self and the mind. At our most basic, each of us is a *Self* that is whole and complete. However, overlying and obscuring the Self, there is an automatic and mechanistic part of us, the mind.

As we enter into the DKDK realm (Don't Know that we Don't Know) where Elder resides, we will find there are blocks to our clear understanding of life. The most basic of these blocks is the mind itself. It is the source of all blocks to becoming clear about yourself, about others, and about life.

Once you gain clarity about how the mind works, there is a shift. You become a person who *has* a mind, in sharp contrast to the usual assumption – that you *are* your mind.

The first step to master this model is to grasp: You have a mind. You are not your mind.

This is a critical statement and should not be read lightly. It is the core of our model.

For now, think of your mind as a filing cabinet, full of information about you – your opinions, your ideas, your likes, your dislikes, and your fears. Its files dictate how you approach life. The mind operates automatically, a mechanical well-oiled machine.

Blindness to Context

In the ordinary course of life, most people are unaware of this automatic aspect of ourselves.

Just as the bird is unaware that air exists because air is the context for the bird, and just as the fish is unaware that water exists because water is the context for the fish, in that same manner humans are unaware of the mind. The mind has, by default, taken over as the context for our lives.

Most of us assume we *are* our minds. This is not so. Until you examine that assumption, the mind will continue to hold you in its command. Living your life inside of the-mind-as-context is incredibly limiting.

Earlier we referred to this Indian Proverb: "There are three Great Mysteries: Air to the Bird, Water to the Fish and Man to Himself."

In this book, I serve as the larger of the flying fish saying, "See. That stuff there!" and point to that which runs you unnoticed – the mind. As the flying fish, I will show you how we will discover how " ... Man to Himself" can become known. And how You can become truly known to You.

See! That stuff down there. It's called Water

How Context Works

Just as water is context for the fish, so the mind acts as context for our thinking and actions.

Diagram #5

How to Discover the Mind

There are some things that can't be seen directly. We can see only their effects. For example, you cannot see the wind, but you can see its effects in the swaying of trees and grasses as it passes. Neither can you see the mind, yet you can become aware of its effects. It babbles. This babbling shows up for you as your internal conversation.

Close your eyes, please, and listen to that internal talk. The mind's babbling might sound like this:

> *What is he talking about ... what babbling ... brooks babble, not me ... I don't hear any talking ... why is he calling me a mind ... I hope the rest of the book isn't going to be like this ... maybe I should go for a walk ... or take a nap....*

Those thoughts *are* the babble. That babble is *the mind* using your voice. We are used to calling these thoughts, "Me, thinking." It is not. It is your filing cabinet of thoughts, automatically running. It is sometimes referred to as "self-talk." I once heard a child refer to it, "I like listening to my own talky-talk."

The good news is once you have discovered this for yourself, you will never be able to *un*discover it.

Who Is Listening?

However, if we ask ourselves, *Who is listening?* the answer is – You.

Other terms for the listener, utilized by spiritual disciplines who deeply understand this powerful model, are the *Self,* the *Being, Essence,* and the *Transparent I.* I shall use *'You'* mostly but occasionally the others, always capitalized.

Believing that this inner chatter is *who you are* is an existential error, one that needs to be corrected in order to see life clearly.

The Mind as Your Enemy

For now, please think of the mind as your enemy. It knows that if you really get this section, it will be exposed. And it does not want to be exposed.

So the enemy-mind may cause you to doze off or drift away. Or it might divert you by wondering what you will have for dinner. It might pull up a scene from a recent movie. It might have you decide this is just *so* boring.

If it brings in any of these diversions, please keep returning to your reading. You may need to force yourself to read on. If you find you cannot stay with this, *have someone else read it to you.* To repeat, the mind, your enemy, does not want you to understand any of this.

Let's give the mind a short break and come at it obliquely.

1975. The Ramada Inn Ballroom; Arlington, Virginia

I first became aware of my mind during my *est* training. The trainer, Stewart Esposito, walked back and forth across the low stage. He spoke to us while alternately writing on a pair of large blackboards. I began to notice a pattern. When he wrote on the left board, I would doze off. When he returned to the right board, I would awaken.

How odd, I thought. *I won't do that again.*

He moved to the left board and I fell asleep again. Only to once again awaken when he moved to the other board.

No! I will stay awake!

Stewart had informed us we would tend to fall asleep when the material got too confronting, but I had assured myself that I, Surgeon Harvey, could confront anything.

I leaned forward and focused intently. Within fifteen seconds he had moved to the left board and, once again, I fell asleep.

What the hell IS this?

I held my eyelids open with my fingers. This time I didn't fall asleep. *But I couldn't read the words.* I looked to the right board and Stewart's handwriting was perfectly legible. I looked at the left board and the letters and words were blurs.

Upset and frightened, I poked the young man to my right and murmured, "Hey, what's on the left board?"

He replied, "How the mind works."

What?

I was shaken. Anything that could make me fall asleep rather than allow me to understand was bad news indeed. This meant I could no longer make the claim that *I* was captain of my fate, the master of my destiny. Something was in charge. But it wasn't ME.

I did not like this one bit.

At that point, I gave up my doctor-knowingness and realized there was something about me, a critically important something, I knew nothing about. Until then I had been arrogant enough, pretentious enough, to think I really *did* know.

I had been so very wrong.

How Your Mind Works

> *"Fasten your seatbelts, it's going to be a bumpy night."* – Margo Channing, *All About Eve*

The belief that you *are* your mind is a hurdle, the first of many. However, it is the highest one.

The mind serves an important purpose; but before we look at that purpose, let's look at how the mind actually works.

The mind is afraid of anything new. It is constantly warning to be careful, *new is bad, different is bad*. For instance, when meeting a new person, the mind might sound like this:

> *Who is this? ... gee, even taller than me ... not good ... but heavier, ten or twelve pounds on me, and not that well put together ... oh oh, looking at me funny ... I wonder if we could be friends ... I don't think so, too wealthy, too attractive, better than me ... And that Rolex ... wonder what that cost ... what a showoff ... I really hate that, it makes me feel small ... I better be careful....*

On and on it babbles, automatic and so always-present as to be unnoticed. Your particular self-talk will differ in content from the above, but the qualities of *comparison* and *watch out!* are always in attendance.

Become an observer of the mind's chatter. Note your particular flavor of that inner-dialogue.

The mind chatters away to try to figure out whether this *thing-right-in-front-of-me* is dangerous or safe. If it concludes a stranger is *better than* me, that's dangerous. Yet, if it concludes that this same stranger is *less than* me, well, that's not good either. The mind, by applying one standard after another to every new person and situation, always comes to this same conclusion – Dangerous! Be Careful!

What the Mind Is Not

The mind has no use for the bond between all living entities. You cannot be intimate with the mind. The mind is an automatic machine and machines are not intimate.

Nor does the mind have principles. It has standards of comparison, standards of what is good and bad and standards of what is right and wrong, but it has no principles. Compassion, intimacy, caring and kindness are foreign to it. Our profoundly human principles do not belong to the mind but to your Being, to Essence, to Self. Principles are the core of You.

The mind's standards can do great damage, preventing true relationship.

By your reading this, you have confronted the enemy. The mind does not like it. If you (your mind) are upset, you may want to write about it. And if you are not upset, beware, for your enemy is clever. It lurks and will show up later.

The mind has been around a long time – your entire life – and is powerful indeed. It has done virtually all of your thinking for you.

The Purpose of the Mind

The mind has a specific purpose: *The purpose of the mind is to cause the survival of the Self* (This is half of it – the good half: the other half is the kicker.) **or anything that the Self considers itself to be.**

As a result of that kicker, there are two critical outcomes:

1. The mind has caused the Self to consider that it IS the mind.

2. Therefore the mind considers its purpose is to CAUSE ITS OWN SURVIVAL.

Stay with me on this. I am the same as you in this regard, for the mind had long convinced me that my mind was who I was. Please read these three bolded sentences over and over until you have them memorized. However, if you can't do that, skip them. Come back later. *(See Notes.)*

Existential Error

The mind has probably convinced you that who you are is the sum of your ideas, your convictions, your thoughts, your conclusions, your standards, and your beliefs. These are not You. These are all aspects of your mind.

It is a basic error – an existential error – to believe that these aspects of the mind are who you are. This error is the source of almost all the difficulties human beings face. The basic truth of being a human being is this: **I am NOT my mind. I HAVE a mind.**

It will help to read this whole section out loud in front of a mirror. Reading it out loud will help you to bypass the mind. I am quite serious.

The Logic of the Mind

The mind is logical. It thinks like this:

I, mind, am the true you.

My job is to cause your (my) survival.

You have survived the past and are alive now.

> *Therefore I have done my job.*
>
> *I conclude that whatever happened in the past is the key to your ongoing survival.*
>
> *All your thoughts, ideas, attitudes, prejudices and assumptions are part of what happened.*
>
> *I will ensure your survival by having only what happened continue to happen.*

I want to emphasize that this mind-logic includes the mind's view that, not only have you survived all the events of the past, so also have your ideas, your convictions, your thoughts, your conclusions, your standards, your beliefs, your opinions, your points of view, your attitudes, and your actions. With those, you have survived. Therefore, those were the *right* ones for your continued survival.

Consider the power of that logic: you were the way you were, you did what you did, and you had what you had. And you survived. So the mind concludes that what you were, what you did, and what you had, *caused* your survival.

Therefore, your mind as your protector, as your survival-insurer, wants you to *be* only those things of the past, *do* only those things of the past, and *have* only those things of the past.

So of course the mind, determined to protect you (itself), is terrified of any challenge or change, simply because it *is* change. "You change, you die," says the mind. Thus change of any kind is a threat. We could say that the mind not only loves the past, it is *addicted* to the past.

The Mind Says NO!

Should you wish to change, the mind will resist. Why wouldn't it? It is, after all, like a fiercely-protective mother. It may postpone, forget, break its word, and be too tired. Or it will tell you, *This is not the right time, sweetie.* The mind has many arrows in its quiver to shoot down change.

The mind is thus a commitment to say NO to whatever is new, unfamiliar, and the slightest bit uncomfortable. The future, being unknown, is a threat.

Become a student of the mind's babble, its talky-talk. Notice your opinions as merely *opinions.* Notice your standards of how you and others should behave as merely *your own standards of comparison.* Notice your conclusions as merely *your conclusions,* rather than as the truth.

Let's interrupt our examination of the mind to look at this question: *"If I am not my mind, WHO AM I?"*

Who You Really Are

You are not some *thing.* Who You are is the context for your life. You are the space within which your life occurs. You are Essence. You are the Listener. Consider that You are a Spiritual Being on a human journey. You are the space of your principles – Intimacy, Caring, Compassion and Kindness. You are also the space of Imagination, Creativity, Genius, Intention and Vision. You are the space of Love.

More About the Mind

The stuff of your life is the content of who you are – your job, your relationships, your car, your triumphs, your failures. Even your mind is a particular piece of content, a huge piece consisting of ideas, opinions, conclusions and standards.

Although your particular mind has the distinct flavor of being your *individual* mind, it is not. There is a collective cultural mind and your individual mind links with that cultural mind almost perfectly. The correlation is so close that it may be accurate to say that almost all your thoughts, ideas, notions, assumptions, evaluations, and standards *are not even yours.* Rather, they belong to a larger mind. You inherited them by being born into them.

This means that it is useful to stop taking our views and opinions so seriously. They may not even be ours, perhaps belonging to our family, to our culture, to our worldview. Thinking of our so-called-personal views, judgments and standards this way makes it easier to examine them and choose whether to retain or discard them.

The Mind's Operating Code

This part is designed to give your mind something to work with. The mind is logical and likes reason and understanding. So let's look at how the logic of the mind works. It has an operating code. The Mind's Operating Code is this: *Everything reminds it of everything else, including detours to other sets of thoughts.* It works automatically and it has patterns.

Automatic Patterns

Neuroscientists tell us our brains consist of repetitive neural pathways of firing neurons. We like to call these *patterns of thinking,* but it is not real thinking. Rather it is one thought, followed by the next thought, the next thought, and the next thought. A pattern is the same set of thoughts being replayed by the mind, the same set of brain neurons firing. It doesn't take much to trigger one of these thought patterns. An emotion, a smell, a glance, and that pattern gets triggered and runs automatically.

There are times when it is easier for us to notice this is occurring. For example, when you find yourself saying, "Sorry, my mind was wandering." At such moments, you can most easily notice the patterns. That wandering was a set of automatic paths which, as you observe them, are consecutive trails of thoughts following the same pathway, with little deviation.

These trails are familiar; none are new. Each thought is from the past. Each pattern is from the past. And each set of patterns is from the past. They are like the well-worn grooves in an old LP record. The mind just kicks in and whips down the grooves of those familiar sets of patterns.

Clever marketers have long known about patterns, developing jingles to associate with their products. For instance, a recent TV commercial for Nationwide Insurance had football quarterback Peyton Manning humming the tune "Nationwide Is on Your Side."

He never spoke the words, but hummed the familiar tune while on the field, eating a sandwich, in the ice tub, and driving. The only connection to the product was the tune. Since I know the tune, my mind keeps running over it.

Pattern, pattern, all is pattern.

Another example of patterns shows up in young men who, with testosterone raging, have a set of patterns which reminds them of sex. This is illustrated by the story of the young man who goes to a therapist.

"Everything reminds you of sex?" the therapist asks.

Embarrassed, the young man replies, "Yes, everything."

Doubtful, the therapist draws a straight line on paper. "What does this remind you of?"

"Sex."

The therapist draws a square and shows it to him.

"Sex," says the young man.

The therapist leans back, "Hmm, you *are* in a bad way."

The young man says, "Hey, I'm not the one drawing the dirty pictures!"

The Mind: The Adult

Once you really get that who you truly *are* is the context for your life, you will become acutely aware that almost everyone assumes they are their mind. And their mind is a fearful mind, fear being the very ground-of-being of the mind.

And fear is the very ground-of-being of Adulthood.

In this book, *mind* and *adult* can be thought of as synonymous. This may not be completely accurate, but it is useful to think of it this way. Doing so will make your process much easier. In that same vein, *You* means your Essence, your Being, and is synonymous with *Elder.* This too is not entirely true, but it is a useful place to stand as you read further.

So we could say that what distinguishes Adult from Elder is the relative role of the mind. The mind is context for the Adult, whereas the Being is context for the Elder. *The mind owns the Adult, whereas the Elder owns the mind.* The Adult is on automatic. The Elder is not. This distinction is as powerful as day and night.

The mind dictates less to the child, particularly the young child. The mind rules more strongly for the Pre-Adult. But for Adult, the mind dictates its world.

Enlightenment

Once you know you *have* a mind and you understand its purpose, many spiritual disciplines would consider you as enlightened. I agree, yet it is not without humor because enlightenment also means to "lighten up." So, even though we have been working with complex material, you might want to lighten up. Remember that Elder also has a sense of humor.

As Werner Erhard, my wisest teacher, once said, "Life is important, but it ain't serious!"

Disengagement

On your path to become an Elder, your primary task is to disengage from that automatic Adult part that has kept you locked into your past emotions, thoughts, attitudes, and actions. You must be free to choose which aspects of Adult to keep and which to discard. You cannot choose, however, if you have not freed yourself from the automatic dictates of Adult, from the automatic dictates of the mind. Fortunately, there is a technology to help you do exactly that. I will present it in further sections.

Let's look at a general life situation and notice how the mind might function. Take upsets, for example.

Upsets

Upsets are based on our past. Upsets, as leading research neuroanatomists recently discovered, have their own powerful repetitive neural pathways. At the time of an upset, if the mind were put on loudspeaker it might sound like this:

> *"Look what just happened. She shouldn't have said that to you. That really hurt your feelings, just like that terrible thing in the past. You survived it that time, but you were lucky. I will go over it all again with you so you can remember how bad it was and how unexpected.... So listen up now; it's for your own good...."*

You are upset in the present by what you *are certain* is a present situation, but is not. Your present upset is an unwitting reminder of an upset in the past.

When you find yourself upset in the present, *you are not upset about what you believe you are upset about.* Rather your mind has diverted you into your past, perhaps from an incident when you were, say, five or six years old.

We will go into this in greater depth later.

Your Mind as Your Servant

Now that we have established the mind as your enemy, let's speak of the senior view – the possibility of the mind as your friend and servant.

Remember that the mind has a job to do – to cause the survival of You. When frightened, the mind will always try to take over. When it does, it reverts to causing *itself* to survive instead of your Essence. Your Being. You.

To keep that from happening, you will need to train it. You will need to assure your mind, love your mind, and thank your mind for doing such a great job protecting you so effectively. You might even wish to give your mind a name. I call mine *Bentley* when it is my servant and friend, and *Crazy Barkley* when it takes over.

Much of your Elder training will be to train your mind to become your servant.

Put the Past into the Past

There are two aspects to your self-training. The first is to release the power of the mind over your life and convert it to your servant. The second is to enhance the power and effectiveness of your Being, your Essence … You.

The largest part of your self-training will be to put the land of the mind where it belongs – *in your past.* The goal is to have a past that merely informs the present, not a past that runs your life.

Putting the past in the past where it belongs will give you the clear space in the present to create the future. If there is no clear space to create, there is no future other than more of the past. As long as your past keeps hooking you, it takes up all the space of the present, preventing you from creating the future.

Putting the past in the past allows the present to be yours, uncontaminated. You will be more able to *Be Here Now.* Further, you will have a clear space to create a future that is bold and creative, a future that will pull you into itself with enthusiasm and joy.

So that's it. That's the model. It is an elegant, useful, and comprehensive model of the way human beings work. It takes persistence to understand it because the mind wants you *not* to understand it. This model provides the underpinnings for the wise saying, *"The Mind is a Terrible Master and a Magnificent Servant."*

Attributes of Elder

Before continuing your Elder training, let's clarify the attributes of Elder. By this I mean the BEING-ness (the You-ness) of Elder.

Attributes of the Being-ness of Elder

Core Attributes:

- Wise
- Compassionate
- Listens Carefully

Other Attributes:

- Joyous
- Open
- Kind
- Generous
- Playful
- Forgiving
- Living in the Now
- Loving
- Vulnerable
- Integrity
- Fully Self-expressed

These are not goals to be reached. These are the natural aspects of our Being, who we are as our birthright.

They are distinct but they are not separable. Our Being is a whole, yet we have different terms to describe aspects of that wholeness. These attributes are our natural bond with others. They are our core, our Essence, our connection with Spirit.

These attributes of being-ness are most fully present in an Elder, who could also be referred to as a *humane becoming.*

Summary of What Is Coming Up

1. You will have reduced the mind's power over you by applying proven techniques to clean up your past.

2. You will have become vulnerable and stopped covering up. You will have become authentic.

3. You will have regained the fullness of your integrity.

4. You will have become ready, able and committed to take responsibility for your entire life – past, present, and future.

5. As a result, you will have created a clear space in present time which contains possibility, wisdom, and a powerful vision for the future. With this, you will have become free. Ah, Elderhood in its fullest.

6. You will have become clear that it is not the past that pushes. It is the future that pulls.

The Past Is Not Solid

There is a particular technology to putting the past in the past. It is called "completing the past" and it is based on the understanding that the past is not solid. Rather, our past consists of a set of incidents and what we concluded those incidents meant.

We created a massive set of explanations so as to make sense of what happened, especially about what others did to us. We also have explanations of what we did to others.

There was *what happened* – the incidents as a set of facts. And there are the stories we told ourselves those facts meant.

However, we do not relate to the past as a set of interpretations. Rather we relate to the past as though that was *really the way it happened.* It was not. To unravel the past and the power it has over us, we need two tools, two distinctions.

The first of these distinctions is called "incomplete experience." The second is "conflation." These are powerful distinctions, rarely spoken of in social circles.

Two Kinds of Experiences: Complete and Incomplete

Reflect on the idea that there are two kinds of experiences, complete and incomplete. Having a *complete* experience of an incident means you have experienced all aspects of it so fully there is no residual emotional charge. It is over and done with. If it remains in memory at all, it is as an insignificant fragment.

To fully experience an experience means to be so completely *in the full truth of its occurring* that it will not function as a pull from the past. The incident has minimal impact on either your present or your future.

By contrast, an *in*complete experience is one where the incident is not fully experienced and has been cut short or aborted. The aborting might have been in the emotional, physical, or mental realm.

Take the common example of a young girl who falls and hurts her knee. She runs to her mother crying with pain and indignation. Mother, noticing it is just a skinned knee, tells her she is just fine. She says something like, "When you run like that, what do you expect?" Then she adds, "You're not really hurt. Be a big girl and stop crying."

Words like this can act as glue, trapping a child in mid-experience. She hurts physically, and now she feels confused, misunderstood and angry. When she tries to make sense of what happened, whatever she decides – about herself, about her mother, about life – might affect her for a lifetime.

Hers was an *incomplete* experience.

Had this girl's mother held her in her arms, expressed her compassion for her pain and indignation, and let her cry it out, it is likely she would have run off to play, not even remembering the episode the next day. The incident would have been non-impactful because she would have been fully present to the reality of the occurrence.

It would have been a *complete* experience – one without impact.

The Power of Incomplete Experiences

We have each had many incomplete experiences over the course of our lifetimes. These have a way of reaching forward from the past and acting as a dark shadow upon our lives, a shadow that strips the color and joy from the present.

Some have had a more profound effect on our present way of being than others. The most powerful have included physical pain, emotional pain, and a threat to our survival. The threat may have been real or only perceived as real, but the impact is the same because perception *is* reality for us.

Some of us, when young, had experiences so horrific we could not confront them. Instead, we buried them deeply.

Our incomplete experiences shape our world. Our lives are created not so much by the actual *facts* of what happened, but by what we told ourselves those facts *meant*. Those interpretations, those stories, are the source of the beliefs we have about ourselves, about others, and about the world. They deeply color the present. Those stories have shaped our attitudes, our opinions, our views, our emotions, our feelings, and our standards.

And, most importantly, they give us a default future that contains nothing but the past.

The Power of Completion

When an Elder has done the work to complete many experiences of the past, she is far less hooked by any residual incomplete experiences and can be more present with herself in her wholeness and thus with others more deeply. She has discovered the source of Freedom and Joy.

Conflation of Fact and Story

"Just the facts, ma'am. Nothing but the facts." – Jack Webb, *Dragnet* TV Show, 1967

An attorney asks us for the facts of a situation. She knows there is the *"who, what and where"* of a situation and she distinguishes them from the witness's opinion, analysis or conclusions. Facts do not include a *"why."* When we mix facts and opinion we are said to conflate them.

Conflation means to join or merge two or more things into a unified whole. We will use the term in the sense of a *mistaken* conflation, those we have joined together *inappropriately.*

Any past incident consists of two aspects: facts and story. Story is what we decided the facts meant – the narrative of our evaluation, analysis, and the conclusions we came to about ourselves, others, and life. The problem occurs when we do not distinguish between the facts of what actually happened, and what we said those facts meant. We conflate the facts and story.

As an example, consider the following: You are standing on a street corner. A bus jumps the curb. It strikes you. Those are the only two facts. But later on, you might tell the story about what happened to yourself and to others like this:

> *Well, there I was, shopping downtown. I was standing on the corner, you know, minding my own business. And there was a red light ... the bus had the red light.*
>
> *Why do you suppose the stupid bus company hired a blind guy to drive a bus? He had to have been blind ... and besides, they never do maintenance on those old buses ... probably the brakes were all shot.*
>
> *Well, anyway, there I was, just about to start across the street when WHAM! That stupid yellow bus just slammed right into me ... right into my side. See, right here? ...*
>
> *Hey, if I had myself a better lawyer, maybe I could've gotten more than the measly couple thousand dollars from their insurance company. You think?"*

And on and on goes that story, being embellished and bone-sucked dry for years.

The Facts: The Story

Fact and story are distinct. By running together (conflating) what actually happened (the facts) and what we said they meant (the story), we fool ourselves. The more we tell the conflated story and the more we listen to ourselves telling it, the more we lose access to the simple facts. And the more *the conflated story becomes real,* we easily convince ourselves *our story is what actually happened.*

Humans tell stories. Stories give our lives meaning, flavor and juice. We are automatic meaning-making machines. This is not wrong: it is just what's so. This storytelling, this meaning-making machinery is a huge aspect of our mind.

Our Life Story is a gathering of such stories. Ultimately we fool ourselves into believing we *are* that large Story, one which may be *completely unrelated* to the facts of our lives.

Personal Example of Conflation: The Hurricane

I was two years and ten months old. It was in the early evening of the beginning of the 1938 New England Hurricane. I was sitting on my father's lap on our open porch. My father commented it was getting dark early. I watched the branches sway on the Norway Maple tree in our front yard.

These are the facts of what happened:

My mother said, "Ralph, bring the boy in."

My father said, "Rose, he's all right here."

My mother said, "I want that boy inside now."

"Oh, all right!" my father said in an angry voice.

He brought me inside.

This is the story I made up: my mother did not

understand me and would keep me from being a real boy; she was the bad one and my father was the only one I could trust. I told myself I had to choose between the two of them. I chose my father at that moment and I divorced my mother.

I never let her back in. I remained so angry at her that I rebuffed her every chance I could. I look back with shame at one particular incident.

The worst expression of my resentment occurred at the age of seventeen. I was confirmed as an Eagle Scout, the first one from our small town. I was one of a group of twenty from our area of Massachusetts. During the ceremony we were each asked to stand to honor our mother and thank her for her role in our lives. I refused to stand. I sat solid as a rock and stared straight ahead. I could hear my mother sobbing. It was the cruelest thing I could have done.

I so believed that story for seventy-five years and so acted out of its "truth" that I grew up motherless. I became angry at all women, I divorced twice, I became sex-addicted, and I lost the respect of my children. My story cost me enormously in terms of intimacy, relationship, and stability. And my actions toward my mother and other women cost me their respect and my self-respect.

Yet it was only a story told by a toddler. But it was a terrible and powerful story that damaged many lives.

Recently, while participating in an Integrity Seminar, I suddenly saw that I had never distinguished the facts from the story. As I separated them, it was as if a light had come on.

Once I had distinguished the two, I made up a more useful story – that my mother loved me, took care of me, and wanted me to be safe. My mother is long dead. I have apologized to her in spirit and will complete doing so when we meet on the other side.

In addition, I have called many I had hurt as a result of that old story and apologized. I forgive myself, yet I still cry when I read this.

There is still the bleed-off of sorrow. I am honoring my mother and apologizing by including her in this book. She held books in awe and I believe she would be glad to be included.

I dedicate this part of the book to Rose, my mother.

Another Personal Example of Conflation: Claudette and the Dime

I fell in love with Claudette Dorothy in the first grade. One day, while behind the rack in the space we called the cloakroom, I heard a coin clink on the floor. I waited until the only other person in the cloak room left. Claudette.

I ran over and picked up the coin, a dime. I spent it at recess on a small balsa airplane. Afterward, I whispered my secret in my teacher's ear.

She announced to the class I had something to tell them. I told the class what I had done. I felt ashamed and humiliated.

Then Claudette said, "I didn't drop any money."

My head whirled with confusion.

I concluded four things: *I can't trust girls; I can't trust teachers; I am a bad person;* and *I just don't understand.* The story I told myself was that I was just not good enough.

I lived from that story for decades.

I didn't revisit this foundation of mistrust and misunderstanding for forty years. But when I did, I separated the facts from the story. The facts were few: *I heard something drop. It sounded like a coin. I found a dime. I picked it up and spent it. I told the teacher. She said, "Harvey has something to tell the class." I told the class. Claudette said, "I didn't drop any money."*

And then there was the story. The one I made up about what that meant. Yet, it didn't live for me as a *story.* Rather it lived as the *truth.* Particularly the conclusion: *I can't trust women.* This evaluation shaped my life, keeping me confused, untrusting, and distant from others.

This story dovetails with the one I made up about my mother.

Now, as an Elder, I can think of a half dozen ways to retell the story with another meaning. Yet, it had taken decades before I was actually able to *take the conflation apart.* Once I did, however, I was able to disempower the false conclusions upon which I had based so much of my life.

Most people have childhood incidents for which they have not forgiven themselves. And we *all* have incidents for which we have not forgiven others.

Might these actually be conflated stories we have been telling ourselves for years?

How much might our lives lighten up by re-examining our stories, many in the form of grudges, old hurts, or long-standing resentments? What if we separated the facts from what we, when younger and less experienced, were so certain those facts meant? And what if we made up a totally different interpretation? What kind of toxic weight might we stop carrying around?

Not All Stories Are Personal

Most of the stories we tell ourselves are not personal. We live inside *stories as reality* our entire lives, not just inside our own personal stories, but within the family stories and, most basic, within the worldview stories. Consider the possibility that culture might be nothing more than a set of agreed-upon stories.

Because these are stories-as-context they are mostly invisible. Cultural anthropologists, when studying a culture, look from the outside and identify these cultural stories as the *myths* of a culture. Both these cultural stories – myths – and your personal stories – also myths – are powerful indeed. They shape your life, for good or for bad.

However distinguished, they can be re-languaged to open life widely. Wisdom, then, is clearly not about facts, but rather about our choices of stories that support and elevate and expand us as *humane becomings* – as Wise Elders.

Shame

Shame is the secret emotion holding many of our conflated stories in place. We are too ashamed to tell them to others, which keeps us stuck.

Shame is universal and one of the pair of background conversations we have not dared to put on loudspeaker. The other is fear.

Shame is distinct from guilt. Guilt is the painful feeling resulting from DOING something wrong. Shame is the intensely painful feeling that we are unworthy of love and belonging, that we *ARE* something wrong.

It is the feeling that I don't belong, that there is something wrong with me. That wrongness is vague, undefined, but terribly powerful. Shame is universal and it must be concealed. No one can ever be allowed to find out. It is a double bind because it is shameful to feel shame.

The inner conversation for shame sounds like:

> *I am not good enough, I don't belong, I am an outsider and I can't tell anyone because they won't understand. I know they couldn't possibly feel this way about themselves, so they would leave me if I confided in them. Worse, my admission that I feel this way would mean I really am this way.*

The inner conversation is sometimes so deep we can't even allow ourselves to know we have it. As

Brene Brown tells us, “It is lethal, it is deadly ... it is universal and we are in it deep. Shame depends on my belief that I am alone. It grows in secrecy, silence and judgment. The less you talk about it, the more you got it....”

We were not born this way, but we may just die this way.

Fear

Fear is the second critical background conversation, one most of us do not share. Fear is another background conversation we have not put on loudspeaker.

But fear is universal. *We are all afraid. And we don't know what we are afraid of.*

This can be a serious problem, especially if we don't realize that others are also afraid. Because if we don't know this, we think our personal fear is ours alone. So we hide it. We deny it. Like I did for forty years.

We Are All Afraid

Fear keeps us perpetually and automatically locked into the stage of Adult. Fear locks us into the *Doing* mode that characterizes Adult. To fully *Be* is to be free of fear. Increasing freedom from fear is one attribute of an Elder.

Fear is not personal to you. It only feels personal, in the same way the impersonal rain feels personal when it gets you wet. Not only does each of us have fear but, devastatingly, like shame, we are fearful of showing it.

If we do not evolve into Elder, we will continue to be fearful until the day we die.

We Pretend We Are Not Afraid

We live within a giant conspiracy in which we all pretend that none of us is afraid. This pretense is part of the Cosmic Egg. To live within our present worldview, however, *is to be afraid.* If you observe your mind in action, there is usually a conversation going on that is fear driven. It may sound something like this: *What if they reject me? What if I fail? What if they find out how scared I am?*

Other conversations float on the surface of the fear. For example: *It's dark and cold outside, so maybe I should stay home where it's safe.*

Or: *I'm getting older, and everyone in my family dies early.*

Each of us has hundreds of these floaters.

Here is the problem: your mind *is* your fear. The mind so wants your survival … it so wants you to live in the past where it is safe … that it is terrified of the future, terrified of *what could happen if … (fill in the blank).* And it is also terrified of *anyone else* finding out it is terrified. Thus we humans continue to live inside an enormous lie. The lie is: "We have it all together."

On Having It All Together

James Howard Kunstler, an author and visionary, has introduced what he calls Kunstler's Law: In any group of a hundred people, ninety-nine will be certain all the others have it more together than they do.

If the ninety-nine are Adult, the one is probably an Elder. Elders know neither they nor the others have it all together. They know they *do not have it all together and never will,* and they find that amusing. In the holding of that paradox, they are not only okay with themselves, but actually love themselves. They love themselves, not in spite of their flaws, but *because of them.* They love themselves just as they are, and just as they are not.

So it is our lies that keep us distant from each other, these lies we don't know how to escape from. Most of us are afraid to talk about our fear, our shame. When we are afraid to tell the truth about either, we must slog through our lives inside the pretense we are just fine. If we are afraid we will be found out, afraid we are insufficient, we feel we must attempt to prove to ourselves and others that we have neither shame nor fear.

This is like carrying a huge boulder in your arms while smiling and asking everyone who sees you struggling, "Boulder? What boulder?"

There is no Elder in this dilemma.

Fear of Death

Carl Jung once was quoted: "I never had a patient over the age of forty whose emotional issues did not arise, at its most basic, from a fear of death."

This makes sense because if you ask an open and vulnerable person about their fears, and you keep asking them, "Yes, and what then?" they invariably will arrive at the following answer: *"And then I would die!"*

This seems to be the fear that underlies all fears, all problems.

It is easy to find evidence to support the idea that fear of death is the most basic fear for all humans. Most people shrink in horror when shown photos of death. It is frowned upon to speak of death at social gatherings. And whenever a death occurs, the culture advises us to prettify it.

We live within a cultural avoidance, perhaps even a cultural terror, of death.

Elder is nearer to the end of body-life than Youth and Adult. One of the jobs of Elder is to confront death up close and personal.

You will die. Unless you have confronted this fact – not as a possibility, not as a *maybe,* not as a *someday,* but as *reality* – you will remain in fear. Your aversion to confronting your ultimate fear will be a barrier in the Elder Path.

Confront Death: Yours

My suggestion is to confront death as an abstraction and your own death as a particular. Read books and articles about near-death experiences and about reincarnation. Watch YouTube videos and TED talks. Confront your own death, discuss it with your spouse and/or children.

After you confront the reality of your own death, your view might shift. You may conclude death is not only confrontable, but even an exciting aspect of life.

Read over Elisabeth Kübler-Ross's Stages of Grief (Appendix 5). If you still find the topic of death distasteful, you might be stuck in Stage 1: Denial.

The Way Out: Re-Creation Causes Disappearance

There is a way out of fear. There is a way out of shame. There is a technology to it and this technology lives at the heart of Elder Training.

The training of an Elder has a goal of becoming fear-less and shame-less. This might seem impossible, but the goal is actually reachable and it will set you free. I am referring to something beyond courage. Courage means to have the fear and do it anyway. What I mean is to actually have the fear disappear. This is a step beyond courage.

We have already examined one of the tools: the De-Conflation of Fact and Story. Now we'll look at another tool: Re-Creation Causes Disappearance.

Most people do not go directly from Fear to Freedom-From-Fear. The path is strangely indirect. *(See Notes.)*

The Power of Paradox

A tourist in New England stopped alongside a corn field and inquired of the farmer, "How do you get to Plainville?" The farmer replied, "Plainville? Well, you can't get there from here."

You can't get there from here? So how *do* you get there? The parable points at the paradox. You can only get more "here." And that's how you get "there."

The way out of the fear is to go into the fear.

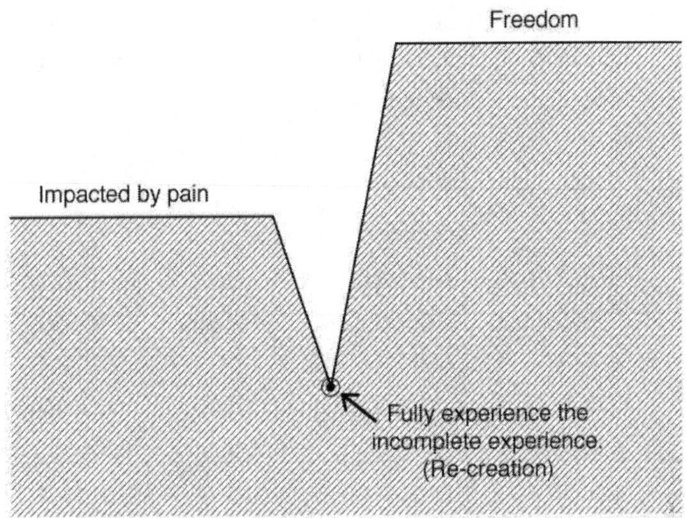

Diagram #6

What this sharp curve points to is this: *You can't simply get better. You must get worse first.*

This curve applies not only to completing the past, but to other aspects of life as well. For example, when you face surgery, *y*ou need to have an operation to become healthy (but you will feel physically worse first). In psychotherapy, the therapist creates a safe space for the patient to dive into emotional pain (and they feel worse doing so) in order to fully re-experience the source and let it go. During massage therapy, the masseuse will make tight muscles hurt in order to release the pain.

The bottom line is, by fully experiencing an incident from the past, the impact on the present can lessen or disappear. The result is freedom from the domination of an impactful *and incompletely experienced* incident.

The Dream

This sharp transformative curve demonstrates our paradox. The paradox can be stated a number of ways. One way is to tell you about a dream.

In the dream, the Secret of the Universe was revealed to me. I instantly awoke and wrote it down. In the morning I couldn't remember what it was, so I looked at the piece of paper. This is what I had written: *Never go upstairs downstairs. Always go downstairs upstairs.*

I felt so disappointed. *Gibberish,* I thought.

Now, however, I am not so sure. When I look at the Curve of Transformation, I wonder whether there might be a requirement to *go downstairs first.*

Another way of stating the paradox is: *You can only go as high as you have been low.* This is the same as: *You can't get there from here. You have to get more here first.*

Look at your past. You have probably had the experience that your efforting did not work. Exerting your will or determining you would improve yourself has not worked. Quitting smoking, losing weight, starting an exercise regime – just make the effort and you'll get it done, right? Wrong. Our efforts overlay what really holds us stuck, like whipped cream on a mud pie.

Completing the Past

The Sharp Curve of Transformation suggests, as have most experienced therapists since Freud, that we need to dive deeper into those stories we tell ourselves about what past incidents mean.

Diving deep into the incident means to first create a quiet physical and mental environment. Once settled, re-visit the incident in its entirety and re-live it within these questions: What is happening ... exactly? What are you seeing? What are you hearing? What are you saying? What do you smell, taste and touch? What emotions are present – go into them deeply and fully, whatever they are – wailing and snotting or perhaps profound anger.

Listen to what you concluded at that time about what the incident means about yourself, about others and about life.

That is what is meant by re-creating the incident. Performing this exercise is one aspect of the larger whole – Completing the Past. By deeply recalling an incident and allowing ourselves to fully experience it, we can minimize, or even completely eliminate, its emotional impact. Here we discover the powerful significance of our axiom, *Re-Creation causes Disappearance.*

In that newly-cleared space, we distinguish facts from story. In that space, we create a new future for ourselves by creating a new and more empowering story.

Here are two additional paradoxes that exemplify that sharp curve.

1. The way to become powerful is to become vulnerable.

2. The way to stop lying is to start telling the truth about your lies.

(See Notes.)

Completing the Past

As we examined earlier, to "complete the past" has a highly-specific meaning.

To *complete* is more powerful than to *finish with.* To complete means *making whole,* with nothing added or taken away. It means to cause a past incident to have little if any impact on either our present or our future. It means to put the past into the past where it belongs so we are able to say, "My past has nothing to do with either my present or my future."

In order to complete the past so it no longer impacts either our present or our future, we must return to our critical incomplete experiences and the stories we told (and still tell) ourselves about what those experiences meant. We complete them by using the particular technology above. To summarize:

1. Fully experience (re-creating) the emotional impact of the incident.

2. Distinguish facts from story.

3. Create a present-time and more empowering interpretation of what happened, one that opens possibility.

This re-creation replaces the damaging interpretations that have dominated our lives. Doing so can cause the impact of those incidents to literally disappear. We do not have to erase our stories from memory. This is not the task. Rather, it is to eradicate their impact, their glue-ness.

This course of action is straightforward. It is also difficult because the mind resists. Remember that the mind lives in the past and wants its vast collection of incomplete experiences and our interpretations to remain intact.

Remember also that the mind has been in charge of your life for decades, and it is used to being in charge. The thoughts passing through an untrained mind are as uncontrolled as a wild puppy. The mind resists discipline, yet it is useless to us if we do not set boundaries for and have it capable of focusing on what we choose.

However, when you discipline (thanking, reining in and reassuring) the mind such that you complete the past, you open up yourself into your inherent wholeness, your inherent You-ness and have the experience of freedom, openness and love.

While the primary task of Elder is to serve others, in order to do so we must begin by serving ourselves (training ourselves) and by that I mean training the mind. If you undertake this self-training, life will open to its full promise. Should you not, then your future will be, by definition merely more of your past.

Cultural Mind

To review, the collective mind of any culture consists of that culture's viewpoints, assumptions, and its complexes of thought, rules and standards of behavior. We were each born into our culture, we live our lives inside it and we die out of it. Yet, the cultural mind continues; it was, is, and will continue to be.

When we assert that we *make up our own minds,* we are fooling ourselves. Most of what we think is actually cultural-think. Little is personal, perhaps less than one percent. Our opinions, views, and standards are mostly not our own, but arise from our past incidents, from our family, our group, our nation, and our worldview. Most are no more personal than the rain that wets us.

These may have originated with the culture, but we do not have to be stuck with them. We can, using certain techniques, disempower them, regardless of whether their source is personal (our past incidents) or from the culture.

Traits of the Mind

Reflect upon this list of the mind's traits. I have put them in loose categories merely for convenience. Doing so might be misleading because the mind consists of mental strings jumbled together like a giant clump of yarn. The strands are distinct but inseparable. When you pull on a strand, others come along. Your mind shifts from one to the others in a split second.

- It's all about me.
- There are winners and there are losers.
- I must win and you must lose.
- I am separate from.
- You are dangerous.
- I already know.

Other Traits:

- Logical
- Unrelated
- Trapped in Dichotomies (either this or that, but not both)
- Oversensitive
- Indifferent to Others
- Righteous
- Invulnerable
- Self-centered
- Blind to Its Assumptions

And it has its conversations:

- You do not care about me.
- If you knew me, you would despise me.
- I must hide myself from you.
- I have no choice.
- Standards matter.
- I am done to by …

And it has its beliefs and standards:

- Circumstances matter.
- Reasons matter.
- Excuses count.
- Proof proves.
- Things *are* a particular way.
- Common sense is real.
- Effectiveness is important.
- Determination works.
- Self-discipline matters.
- There is not enough time.
- If everyone knows then it must be true.
- *Why* is a legitimate question.

And it has its rules for others:

- You should love me.
- You shouldn't hurt me.
- I deserve.
- Everyone knows that.
- I know and you don't.
- You can't boss me.

And it has its evaluations*:*

- I am a failure.
- I am a success.
- I am worthless.
- I am OK and will prove it.
- I am not OK.
- I am not good enough.
- I am nothing.

And it has its comparisons:

- You have it together and I don't.
- I am as good as you.
- I am better than you.
- I make money, you don't.
- I am more attractive.
- I am less attractive.
- I have better kids.
- There is a right way and a wrong way and I do it the right way.

These are all conversations of the mind. If you cannot acknowledge having such thoughts, the mind is doing its job – resisting. Read them again later. You might take a moment to thank your mind for having such traits in order to protect you.

These traits are not *You.* An Elder has all of these and can 'fess up to having them. By contrast, the Adult is dominated by them. The Elder has these traits – as content. These traits devour the Adult – as context.

These mind traits are either variations on the basic conversations of shame and fear, or they are conversations designed to camouflage these two. All are a function of the cultural mind. These traits were present before we were born and they will be here after we die.

They are neither personally yours, nor are they a reflection of bad character. Most of us spend an enormous amount of energy concealing these traits in the mistaken belief they *are* personal and reflect badly on our character.

Notice that the mind reveals itself in the linguistic world of dichotomies (either this or that, but not both). The mind's conversation has three major dichotomies: *good/bad; better than/less than; success/failure.* These dichotomies are aspects of the world of You OR Me, minimal in the early years of Youth, increasingly prominent as one becomes culturally adapted, and virulent in Adult.

There Is Nothing Wrong with You

In those areas where you may be scared, hesitant, or contained, such tentativeness is a product of the cultural mind, not your own. Your fear is not your own. It is universal.

What also is universal is how hard we all work to cover up the fear. This keeps us from knowing one another. It keeps us separate.

Most of Your S… Just Ain't Personal

Where you are intolerant, where you are condemning, where you are judgmental – this is the cultural mind. You have bought into it, and this is as the mind says it is supposed to be. It happened to you unknowingly, unwittingly, and by default. You grew up within the immaturity of our culture with its competitive and distancing worldview of OR.

So, in your Elder Training, do give yourself a break. *There is nothing wrong with you.* No matter what you may believe, no matter what someone has told you to the contrary, you are a *perfect product of our culture.*

Purpose of the Cultural Conversation

This seems a truism: The purpose of the cultural conversation is to *maintain the cultural conversation.* It is the macro version of the perverted purpose of the mind – to cause its own survival.

The Work

The bottom line regarding the path of Elder is that you must do the work on yourself. You can't do the work on the culture because you do not interact with the culture, you only interact with other individuals. And you happen to be the individual you interact with the most. This is why you work on you.

Bad news, I suppose. But this *is the way it is*. So, work on yourself so that *your* world will shift. Out of that, *the* world will shift.

The Work Will Set You Free

Work is the right word here. Sometimes we call it *The* Work. It is not called *play* because the work is to train your mind and your mind does not want to be trained. The mind is smart, it is secretive, it is elusive, and it is tricky. To train it, you must use discipline and perseverance, and you will have to do so for the rest of your life.

To be Elder is to be constantly training your mind.

Your mind will tell you I am belaboring the point. Yes, I am. My intention is to write it so many times and in so many ways that the mind will allow the words to slip in a bit more each time.

You Can't Get There from Here

Remember, you cannot simply shift from *here* to *there.* Take *intolerance* for instance.

You cannot say, "I shall become more tolerant" and have it become so. Rather you must tell the truth by diving deeply into those places where you are intolerant, those places where you are righteous, those places where your standards tell you others have lower standards, those places where you feel superior.

If you do not deliberately do this, you will gloss over your own intolerance and not notice those places where you think or speak detrimentally of yourself and others. Such speaking and thinking are valuable signs pointing to the intolerances of your mind.

You must observe your own intolerances and lay claim to them. *You must be willing to own them.*

You were not born intolerant, you were born *into* being this way. It is irrelevant whether you approve or disapprove of being intolerant. You might note with amusement that you are *intolerant of your own intolerance.*

You have the opportunity to dive deeply into every one of those traits of the mind. To become vulnerable, for instance, you must *stop denying.*

You can become a truth-teller, a teller of the truth about yourself. No more hiding. No more pretending others don't know about your traits of the mind.

Secrets

As an Elder, you do not have secrets worth keeping. The cost is too great. Yet, you are certain you do. It is this certainty that would keep you stuck in Adult and block your entry into the stage of Elder. As an Elder, you *do* have secrets worth sharing.

One major aspect of your self-training is to acknowledge all your negative traits, claim them, befriend them, and find them amusing. You will need to become delighted with your own so-called negative traits. As Werner Erhard said, "The Truth will set you free. Piss you off, but set you free."

It works to fess up and share our truths with another. That old saw *still waters run deep* is simply not so. Still waters run *putrid.*

You can give up your oh-so-special secrets by telling on yourself. A secret told is a secret no longer. On the whole, nobody but you cares about your secrets. Find some way to get those boulders off your back by spilling them to someone you trust. Or anonymously to a stranger.

I had a pair of T-shirts made. On the back they say, "I am an Elder. I will listen to you." On the front is the same and adds, "Say Hi and … start speaking…."

I have discovered that when someone wants to unburden, they say something like, "Hey, cool shirt." "Yes," I say. I look them in the eye and quietly ask, "What secret would you like to tell me?"

The most recent, a muscular man in his mid-twenties blurted, "I am an athlete and I am really good at sports, but I am afraid of … everything!" He threw his arms around me and sobbed into my shoulder. I held him. After a moment, he quieted, pushed away, eyes wet, "Hey, thanks, man." "You're very welcome." An Elder moment.

Once you tell those terrible secrets, you will no longer waste your life hiding them. They no longer have power over you. And you will have freed yourself from another set of mind-chains that are keeping you shackled to the past. Be warned, however, that upon telling them, you also give up using them as an excuse to not be great.

Inauthenticity

One time I was attending a seminar. The leader told the group in a loud voice, "Harvey is the most inauthentic human being I have ever met."

My internal reaction was anger and resentment. My mind spoke loudly, *Who do you think you are to say that about me? I am a famous surgeon!* I said nothing, but I wanted to run from the room in humiliation.

Instead, I did not react automatically. I responded instead. My response was to consider the possibility I just *might* be "that most inauthentic human being."

Since I had granted her the right to coach me, I did something uncharacteristic. For the next month, I introduced myself by saying, "Hello, my name is

Harvey. I am the most inauthentic person you have ever met."

With this choice of action, I became authentic about my own inauthenticity. *And that is as good as it gets.* This daring action, performed in the face of the cultural agreement to never say anything so self-debasing, set the stage for me to become more vulnerable. Even though I could not have named it at the time, it was the action of an Elder-in-training.

Once you take action to free yourself, something happens. You begin to notice that so-called negative emotions and thoughts are there simply to be noticed. When they continue to show up, you can pause, laugh and allow them to be there. You can share them with another and keep on going with your Elder work.

Such pausing, noticing, chuckling, and sharing *is* the Elder work.

There is a feeling of great relief to discover that whatever you have been covering up is no big deal. But the discovery only comes *after* you fess up. Prior to this, your secrets own you and are a big deal indeed.

Noticing Is the Key

There is magic in noticing. This is one of the keys to Elder Training.

First you notice. Observe what happens when you apply *noticing* to an aspect of being human that we just don't want to talk about – lying. By *lying* I mean "to speak something the way it is not."

For instance, when you are upset and someone inquires "How are you?" and you reply "Fine," you are speaking it *the way it is not.* It is a lie. Your reasons why you said it are not relevant.

Lies like this are culturally acceptable. We even have a term for them: *white lies.* You tell them. We all have.

Notice what it is like to read that I believe *you* lie. *Notice* the emotional reaction you might have. Does it, perhaps, show up as anger at feeling falsely accused?

We all lie, we pretend we don't, and we ignore the impact. We fool ourselves. This combination is pervasive and insidious and it is a denial that robs us of our power. Elders must be able to distinguish telling the truth from telling a lie. It is not a good thing for an Elder to have diminished power. I am not saying that it is morally wrong to tell a lie, but I am pointing out that it doesn't work.

Commit yourself to take notice of the lies you tell. Perhaps you will notice a lie called, *I don't lie.*

All Humans Lie

One who speaks a lie is *not* a liar, but is merely one of us (all of us) who speaks something the way it is not.

However, during your training as Elder, reflect upon the notion that white lies are lies. You do not need to hold anyone else to this standard. It is *you* who are in Elder-training, not they.

I am not suggesting you stop telling lies. This would be a mistake. But there is great value *in the noticing,* and you can't notice when you lie if you are focused on *not* lying.

A lie is a distinction, not a negative evaluation. And noticing is always the first step to working with a distinction.

The Golden Road of Noticing

Noticing your lies, and noticing all your other mind traits, is the golden road in. This is the path, the route you take to Elder.

Notice, for example, how *invulnerable* you are. You have been long-trained by the culture to be the Teflon woman or man. By deflecting, you are protected against either real or perceived hurt. Notice how *pretentious* you can be, pretending to be other than the flawed and strange and oh-so-human being you are.

Notice that virtually everything on the list of traits applies to some of your thinking or to some of your actions. Particularly notice the ones you find especially distasteful, to which you want to respond: *Hell, no, that's not me. I can't stand people who do that!*

Also notice which traits you have kept secret. You will need to be willing to become aware that your mind has been hypocritical, false, insincere, deceitful, disingenuous, duplicitous, treacherous, phony, and inauthentic – all the stuff of being a human being who has a mind.

Like all of us.

Notice how the items on the mind traits list show up for you. Do some show up as indictments? As secrets? As idiosyncrasies? Do you find yourself denying you have them?

Consider that these reactions might actually be clever techniques on the part of the mind to keep you living in the familiar past.

It is critical to remember that it is not You that has the traits, but your mind.

Noticing has been the golden road since the beginning of time. It is the path of maturity; it is the Path of the Elder. Further, it is the path of the saints, of the Priest and Priestess. It is the Road Less Traveled.

The golden road is not a linear path; it wanders about. The good news is, regardless of this wandering, you can *be* Elder, *do* Elder actions, and *have* Elder-ness at the same time you are working to own your Adultness, your traits of adult.

The traits on the list will never disappear. They will always be part of you. The difference between being Adult and being Elder is this: Adult is unconscious to itself, whereas Elder is both *conscious of and responsible for* its own Adultness, for their traits of the mind.

Exercises to Free Yourself

There is another paradox. When you train yourself, you must utilize certain traits of Adult – determination, effectiveness, efficiency, self-discipline, and persistence. Some call it "grit." However, when you support others in their self-training, you utilize the attributes of Elder – compassion, kindness and other-oriented, among them. In other words, be rigorous with yourself and compassionate with others.

When you examine the Traits of the Mind list, it is clear we have covered but a few of the traits of Adult. All are available for you to work with. You can choose to actively work with some and allow others to passively accompany. You might choose to work with those to which you have the most aversion, the ones you have the most emotional charge. If not, don't worry, it is fine to pick the low-hanging fruit.

So far we have spoken about how to train the mind in general terms. It's time to get specific about the Elder-training techniques within this technology.

Exercise #1: Traits of the Mind

Step 1. Choose a Trait

It doesn't really matter which one you choose. It is more important that you do the exercise. You might choose one by noticing what easily upsets you or by becoming vulnerable enough to ask a friend what to work on. Whatever your friend tells you will be spot on.

Another way to select a trait is to listen to certain key phrases you tell yourself – *ought to, should, shouldn't, I hate, if only, what's the matter with them,* and any others that say something *should be other than the way it is.*

Notice when you become irritated, upset, or angry. Notice when you replay conversations in your mind or when you can't sleep. Notice when you find a person or a type of person annoying.

Or you might simply note which unpleasant memories keep coming up. If none do, ask your mind to bring up an unpleasant memory. Your mind will be pleased to throw a few at you. Just pick one, it doesn't matter which. You don't have to go for the biggie.

Step 2. Give a Title to the Incident or Trait, and Write It Down

This is more important than it seems. Giving something a name makes it real for you, taking you from the stands onto the court. And writing it gets you into the habit of writing rather than *just thinking about it,* a useless endeavor that will take you nowhere.

Also, writing settles the mind. *Oh, thank you for writing it down,* says the mind. *Now I don't have to protect you by keeping that piece in the forefront. Since we wrote it down, I can relax, for I know it is solidly somewhere.*

A title gives the incident or trait an existence other than in the mind. Titling has it become a specific thing, something you can work with, easier to own.

Step 3. Relax, Let the Images Flow Uncensored

Step 4. Slam Write

Emotional writing is designed to clean out everything the mind says. Slam writing means writing fast, without judging or critiquing or controlling what you are writing.

Write whatever comes up. Don't bother with punctuation, don't worry about grammar or spelling. Write freely. Your writing can be full of cursing and totally irresponsible. Paper may rip; snot may fly; tears may flow.

You might be furious, or intensely sad – just slam whatever you are thinking or feeling onto paper or the computer screen. If it is there as a thought, write it down! Think of it like uncontrolled vomiting. You don't care where the damn stuff lands. Just let it out!

Your writing might be quick, brief. Or you might think it will keep coming out forever. It will not. It is finite, not infinite. Suddenly there will be nothing more to write and you will be clear that you are complete. You might even find yourself laughing.

Step 5. Thank the Mind

You have relieved your mind of a burden. The more times you do this exercise, the more willing the mind is to be a Bentley rather than a Crazy Barkley.

Step 6. Thank Your *Self*

You have done a magnificent piece of work.

As an aside, you might choose to not save your writing. It is not deathless prose; and private writings have a tendency to be discovered and read by others.

Exercise #2: Past Incidents

"All suffering is contained in a story."
– Rod Schwarz, Attorney

The following exercise is a technique to straighten the clump of yarn that has become your story, that story about why *you are the way you are.* A yarn-clump only begins to untangle when you have a pair of ends under control. The two ends are labeled Fact and Story.

Step 1. Choose Something That Happened

Choose an incident to work with. Start with the earliest incident you can remember. Often, the first incident the mind will allow to arise is not the key one. Ask it for "an earlier incident, please."

Step 2. Write the Story As You Have Always Told It

Make no attempt to write it "right." Just write it down the way you have always told it. Include all the reasons, the way it should have been, what you said it meant, plus everything you thought about it, including all the associated emotions you may have felt.

Don't worry about a proper order. Just write what shows up. Slam the desk, let the tears flow. Do not pretend to be nice or reasonable.

When you are done, dry your tears and wipe your nose. Good job.

Step 3. Distinguish Fact from Story

Go back over what *actually happened,* distinguishing the *facts.* Separate the *facts* from what you told yourself they meant – the *story.*

Step 4. Write the Actual Facts

The facts are relatively few and are usually in the realm of action. Including speech action, as in, *she said, then I said, then she did, then I did....* You might include what you saw, heard, said, felt, smelled, touched or had a thought about.

Keep stripping away story remnants until you are left with the barest minimum of facts, cleansed of interpretation, cleansed of story.

Step 5. Write the Story Now Distinguished (Deconflated)

Now write the conclusions (the analysis, the evaluation, the meaning) that you came to *at that time.* You will then have two useful pieces of writing:

1. The facts.

2. What you told yourself *back then* the facts meant – the story.

You should now be clear these are NOT the same. You had them conflated.

Step 6. Create Different Stories to Account for the Facts

This is now child's play. You become *as a child* ("And a little child shall lead them.") and make up a different story.

Create a story that gives you freedom or joy or power. Write it down for clarity. Make up a second one. Make up a third, a silly one.

The only story that is true *is the one you say is true.* So make up your own story. This is what human imagination and creativity are for. Choose an empowering story that gives you freedom and possibility as an Elder.

You are now free. You have freed yourself from the domination of the story you made up as a young person. Back then you said it meant one thing. Now, older and with broader understanding, you can choose it to mean something entirely different.

You have become clear that *you* are the author of the story. In fact, you are the source of *all* the stories of your life.

Moreover, you can now entertain the powerful possibility you are the source of your entire *Life-As-a-Story-You-Made-Up.* Such clarity is the space for an Elder to stand, wiser, more compassionate and less judgmental.

And, as an Elder-in-Training, you can create a story of *your future-as-an-Elder.*

Step 7. Thank the Mind

You have relieved your mind of a burden. The more times you do this exercise, the more willing the mind is to be gentle with you, a smooth Bentley rather than a stupid-ass Crazy Barkley.

Step 8. Thank Your *Self*

You have done a magnificent piece of work.

Now, discard what you wrote. Let the crumpling and dropping of the paper in the trash basket be a metaphor for putting the past into the past where it belongs.

Exercise #3: When Crazed

You know you are crazed when the same thoughts go around and around in your head. Or when you are upset and you can't go to sleep because the story in your mind continuously whirls. Or when you feel like your thoughts are out of control and you can't shift into a calm place.

You know exactly what your flavor of crazed is.

Here is what you can do to help yourself. First, go to the mirror and tell the truth. Look into your eyes and say, "We are crazed right now. I love you. We will get sane together."

Next, go to your computer or grab a pad of paper. Close your eyes and take five big, slow breaths. Open your eyes and start writing. Write as fast as your fingers will move.

Your first words should be: *I am crazed right now.* Then let yourself write whatever comes to mind. Let the words pour out, the misspellings and swear words and tears. No need for punctuation, no need for editing. Your English teacher won't give you an "F." Just vomit it onto the paper.

Do it fast and do it sloppy. Get it all down. Do not pretend to be nice, do not be civil. Blame everyone and everything. Go ahead and cry, slam your hand on the desk. Bring up the fury, the grief, whatever is in there. And write it down!

You will know you are done when you go to write the next thing you are upset about and there is nothing more to write. Now you can sit back and just *be* for a bit. You might be sobbing, you may feel empty. You have gotten it all out. Praise yourself for doing such good work.

Discard what you wrote.

Exercise #4: Voice Dialogue

You can create a future from nothing. You can do this anytime. You do not have to wait until you think you have done enough Elder training to put the past in the past.

Ordinarily, two people are necessary for an effective dialogue, yet there is another paradox. It is possible to have an effective and profound dialogue *between one person.* A dialogue between the Self and the mind. (You know how to do this, for you do something like this all the time as you walk around – and talk to yourself. This exercise is merely more structured.)

This particular technique is based on the notion that when you take a stand for something or create a declaration for your future, the mind will immediately call up the opposite.

Step 1. Choose one from the list of the Attributes of Elder earlier in this book.

Step 2. Create two columns, A and B. You may use a pad of paper or a computer spreadsheet. I prefer an Excel spreadsheet.

Step 3. If your choice was, say, *Generosity,* write a short positive statement in Column A about that trait. Such as *I know myself as a generous person* or *I love my generosity* or *I am always generous.* It will feel right when you have the wording right.

Step 4. Take deep breaths until you feel centered. Close your eyes. Listen to what the mind says in reaction to your declaration. Write that short statement in Column B without censoring it in any way.

Step 5. Again write the *identical* declaration in Column A. Write in Column B what the mind says *this time* in reaction. It will probably be negative. As you repeat this pair of steps, over and over, you will hear the mind come up with a series of objections and negativity.

You will notice something interesting occur. The mind's objections get weaker and weaker until they gradually come into agreement, either smoothly or in fits and starts.

Step 6. When the mind gives consistently positive responses in column two, declare the exercise complete. Thank the mind for its cooperation and acknowledge your courage for doing the exercise.

As a side benefit, when you scan the entries in Column B, you are likely to find indicators of areas for future work. I have found it useful to use this exercise of many of the Attributes of Being.

Meditation Trains the Mind

Meditate. It works. While there are many forms of meditation, I use the Counting Breaths Meditation.

I sit comfortably and close my eyes. I focus on my breathing and count each breath. When I have finished, I open my eyes, declare I have had a successful meditation, stretch, and get on with my day.

The purpose of this meditation is both to observe the mind operate and to train the mind to hold focus. *It is not about quieting the mind.* Rather, your goal is to get to know the mind and train it. As you do, the mind will, over time, quiet itself.

A successful breathing meditation will look like this: You give your word to yourself that you will sit, close your eyes, and focus on your breathing for 100 breaths (or 200 or 500, your choice). Then you keep your word to do exactly that.

Such a simple meditation is a success because you *reached your number.*

However you only reached that number after the mind led you on its merry chase, which may have included dozing off, losing the count, thinking about your day, and planning a menu.

You kept bringing your Crazy Barkley mind back to the count. Whenever you lost count, you simply continued with the last number you remembered. And you said *thank you* each time the mind allowed you to return to your count. Finally, you reached your declared number.

Success!

It is as simple as that and it is as difficult as that. Every time you meditate, you will train your mind to loosen its lifelong grip a little more. When you meditate, you have a great opportunity to observe your mind run its patterns.

It helps to discipline your mind by meditating every day. You do not need a quiet place, nor do you need the additional distraction of a noisy one. Your mind is distractible enough without adding to it. The tighter your discipline, the cleaner the training ground to bring your mind under the dominion of You, your Self.

Count on meditating for the rest of your life.

Any Activity Can Be a Meditation

Any repeated set of actions may be converted to a meditation. For example, when I was a young surgeon I created a *getting dressed* meditation.

In the world of surgery, there is a background understanding that a master surgeon is also a rapid surgeon. I mean *rapid* not in a hasty sense, but in the sense that every motion counts. This is so that our patients are not kept under anesthesia unduly long.

I intended to train myself to become a master surgeon. I knew intuitively I had to make each move count so my hands and my mind would become my coordinated servants. I decided to watch my every move to discover unconscious hesitations or unnecessary motions. This is akin to a professional speaker eliminating from his speaking each *you know, uh,* and *well.*

I would enter the surgical dressing room and change from street clothes into operating room greens in slow motion. This was my meditation:

> *I open my locker (slowly), taking the lock in my left hand (slowly) and using the right thumb and forefinger to (slowly) twist the dial. I apply this s-l-o-w observing intent to the entire dressing process. Focused, I become oblivious to my surroundings, focusing on only one motion at a time.*

When dressed for surgery, I would return to the ordinary state of mind. Looking about, I would often discover that other surgeons who had entered the room at the same time as I were no further along in their dressing than I. Although I had moved slowly, I had wasted no motions. We arrived at the same point at the same time, the difference being that I had dressed with conscious intent rather than automatically.

Encouraged after experimenting with this for several months, I carried the slow motion into the operating room. The intense focus now shifted to a surgical meditation. This had three benefits: I learned to focus my mind on the task at hand without being distracted; I eliminated wasted motion; and I became a rapid surgeon.

Thus I benefited; my mind benefited by being reassured I was safe; and my patient benefited from a reduced anesthesia time.

Create Your Own Meditation

You also can create opportunities to meditate. You train your mind to hold focus at will – while gardening, sewing, exercising or listening to music. Your trained mind becomes your friend and your servant. Your mind, now trained, wants what *You* say is best for you. Now it is You who makes the determination, not your mind.

Be sure to take care of Bentley, who now delights in serving you. Because uncared for or untrained, Bentley will revert to Barkley, wild puppy.

Integrity

The term *integrity* is in a state of flux.

It has been considered to be a kind of uprightness, residing in the realm of cultural morality and honesty. It has also been applied to one who consistently lives within the law.

For many, though, integrity points to something more profound than these loose and insufficient definitions. Others, expressing the same, have added a term to make the distinction stronger, coming up with *profound* integrity or *secondary* integrity.

Joseph Wesley Matthews gave a talk in 1977 at the Maliwada Development Training School, India, later transcribed, in which he spoke of Integrity with great power, referring to its basis as a "destinal resolve," strong indeed.

Landmark has utilized this profound meaning in its courses. I have also incorporated this meaning into my life and speak of it in that sense, its bedrock sense.

This material is more fully elucidated in the seminal monographs by Michael Jensen, Werner Erhard, et al. *(See Notes.)*

Integrity is the bedrock of Elder.

All else rests upon it. Integrity refers to wholeness in the same sense that a circle is whole, complete, and without gaps. There is a wholeness to being an Elder, a completeness. Elder acts with integrity and embodies integrity. Elder *is* integrity. One can grow old without integrity, but one cannot be an Elder without integrity.

Two Layers

There are two layers to integrity: The upper layer of integrity is that you keep your promises and your agreements, including doing what you know is expected of you. In practice, this means you *do what you said you would do by the time you said you would do it.*

At a more profound level, integrity means *who you are is your word. It means to honor your word as yourself.*

Integrity is distinct but inseparable from *responsibility* … in the same sense that the front of the hand and the back of the hand are distinct, but inseparable. You cannot have the front of a hand without a back. Where one is, so is the other.

Conversely, where one is not, the other is not as well. This is the relationship between integrity and responsibility – where one is, so is the other. Where one is not, neither is the other.

Early on in reading this book you made the declaration, *I am an Elder.* As such, you gave your word. This is akin to the biblical, "In the Beginning there was the Word." Word is the source of all.

Who I AM Is My Word

As an aspect of Spirit, word is the source, your source. And who you *are* is who you *declare yourself to be.* You have declared yourself an Elder. This is your opportunity to also declare that *who you are is your word.*

You can do this in front of your mirror by standing there and saying out loud: "Who I Am Is My Word." Repeat this until the one in the mirror gets it.

Having made both of these declarations, "I am an Elder" and "I am my Word," you as a person of integrity take responsibility for every word that comes out of your mouth. Along with this comes the possibility of taking responsibility for every choice you have made, and therefore for how your life has turned out.

If you are not ready for this exercise, wait. We will come back to responsibility later on in the book.

This is from Doug Plette, master business consultant:

> *Your thoughts come and go. Your emotions come and go. You have little, if any, control of either. However, the words you speak? Over these you have total control.*

What Integrity Is Not

Adult, in general, has a particular relationship to Integrity. It is a relationship of convenience. It is an easy and flexible relationship: *I keep my word when it is important to me to do so and ignore it when it is not.* Or: *If I don't keep my word, I have reasons why I did not.* Further: *I excuse myself by being nice, by being sincere, by smiling and by pretending I have integrity.*

Clearly there is neither wholeness nor count-on-ability with such a paltry relationship to your word.

Adult may assume that integrity is the same as *morality.* Wanting to be thought a moral person, Adult believes keeping one's word is good and breaking it is bad. Individual morality and cultural morality both proclaim that keeping your word is the *right* thing to do.

However, integrity is distinct from morality. Integrity is integrity. There is no rightness/wrongness to integrity. That particular dichotomy lives within the realm of morality, not integrity.

Integrity is not the same as *legality* either. Adult may assume: *If I follow all the laws, I have integrity.* Not so.

Adult might also assume integrity is the same as *sincerity.* Sincerity of expression and demeanor is not the same as integrity. It has no rigor. It is like a social grease, enabling us to slide by one another – without integrity.

Conflating integrity with morality or legality or sincerity is not wrong, merely insufficient. Doing so is a junior grade of thinking, a trait of Adult rather than Elder. Neither morality nor legality nor sincerity approach the rigor of Integrity.

No Gaps

Just as there is no integrity to a circle if there is a gap in it, neither can integrity be present if there are gaps anywhere. There is no "kinda" integrity. There is no casualness to it. At any given moment, one is either *in* integrity or *out of* integrity. It is an on/off thing. There is no gray area of *I have integrity everywhere except, well, here.* Integrity has that kind of rigor.

And when one is out of integrity, one is out of integrity. Nothing more, nothing less.

Elder has integrity not only as bedrock, but as the very context of life. Integrity means to honor one's word as one's Self. While integrity means more, much more, than keeping one's word, nonetheless integrity rests upon this foundation.

Keeping one's word is very straightforward: *Do what you said you would do by the time you said you would do it.* What could be clearer? Be impeccable with your word. It is the straight path to integrity.

Without this as the cornerstone, you are out of integrity. This is so important it is worth speaking the converse: Whenever there is difficulty in life, whenever things seem hard, whenever there is a non-workability, take the stand that the source is a lack of integrity *on your part.* It is neither the other person nor the other situation that is out of integrity. It is *your* integrity that is out.

Though the truth of this statement may not ring true in every situation, it is useful to hold it *as though* it were completely true. This provides a powerful place for you to stand as you examine the situation.

When you hold the possibility, that is *you* who is out of integrity, then you can use every issue, every problem, every stuckness, every struggle, every conflict and every bad memory as an opportunity to clean up the past by telling the truth about what *you* did, and, by so doing, come back into integrity.

The mind will not like this. It might react:

> *WHAT! That's BS! It was almost totally THEM. It wasn't my fault. They did it, not me. I just did (or said) what I did to get even. And besides, what I did was so small compared to the big thing THEY did (or said). After all, a relationship is a 50/50 thing and they should be the one to apologize. I am the aggrieved one!*

Well, how's that working out for you? What's your experience when you tell yourself this? Do you feel open and free and enthused? Not likely. Remember, the mind wants you to stay in the past, which means keeping the mess *totally in place.* This is akin to living in a penitentiary whose walls you constructed yourself.

One Hundred Percent Responsibility

The idea that relationships are 50/50 is a lousy theory made up by someone to justify a lousy relationship. Holding firm to that idea is just a place to hide.

The reality is this: If you want your relationships to be full of joy, enthusiasm, and fun, take one hundred percent responsibility for them. If you want your family to work, take one hundred percent responsibility for that happening. The quality of your relationships is up to only one person – you.

As a personal example, I had been living inside a low-grade background resentment that my children hadn't called me. *It is the children's job to stay in touch with their parents,* my mind kept saying. I started to think badly of them.

Before I went too far down that path, I stopped myself. I realized that if I wanted a great relationship with my children as an aspect of my extraordinary life, it was my job to take total responsibility for the relationship. After all, I am the one self-training, not them. I saw that having a great relationship with each of my children was more important to me than the reasons I had told myself for the not-so-great relationship.

So I called each of them and engaged them in conversation. After each call, I felt better about myself and better about them and I was pleased I had called. We got back into communication because *I* reached out. This was more satisfying than remaining in righteousness and resentment.

Right? Or Great?

In this instance, I gave up being *right* and traded it for workability. We always have this choice. We are always in the asking place of, *"Do I choose to be right or do I choose to have a great relationship with X (fill in the blank)?"*

In the situation with my children, I brought myself back into integrity, into wholeness, by restoring the integrity of each of those relationships.

Promises Past

A promise is your word in the world. It is *your* word, whether spoken silently or spoken aloud, whether given to another or given to yourself. It may be a foreground promise or a background promise. All are grist for the mill in cleaning up your past.

Anyone who has cleaned up all the promises and agreements broken in the past is a free person. And a free person lives in the space of possibility. This is that clear space – the space of creativity and the space of co-creation with others. It is the space of the possibility of making a real difference.

It is the space of Elder.

Promises Present

Keeping your promises and agreements is the *foundation* of integrity. To keep your promise is *to do what you said you would do by the time you said you would do it.* It also has a corollary – do what you know is expected of you. Whether you have a spoken agreement about that expectation is not important, for your silence may well be your affirmation that you know of the background expectation, and you will meet it.

Honor Your Word

However, keeping your promises and agreements is not integrity itself. Integrity itself is the *Honoring of your Word* as who you are, as your Self. This is a powerful stand. This does not mean you will always keep your word. Life doesn't work that way. Nonetheless you can always *honor* it.

Honoring your word gives instruction how to handle it when you must break your word. It is possible to break your word and still be within the realm of honoring your word.

Whenever you find yourself in a position when you cannot keep your word, you have three options: keep your word, renegotiate it, or break your word. Each of these has consequences, both immediate and over time. These are not back doors and should not be read as such. This is Elder material at a high level.

As a baseline, when you keep your word in all matters, you can be counted on and you have a reputation for integrity. You consistently make promises and fulfill them, creating a condition of mutual satisfaction.

When, however, you, now known as count-on-able, realize you are unable to keep a promise, you have the option to *renegotiate* it in such a way that, while there will be some impact, you can lessen its severity.

However, if you discover your only recourse is to *break* your word, there is both a short-term impact and a long-term impact. The short-term impact is that you create an upset to clean up. The long-term impact is distrust. It takes so much more effort and commitment to clean up long-term distrust that you might later wish you had moved Heaven and Earth to keep the promise.

Renegotiation

To renegotiate your promise, communicate prior to the deadline:

- Speak precisely the promise you made.
- Request the other person accept an altered promise.
- If agreed, ask what is wanted in exchange for the altered promise.
- Produce it.
- Make the altered promise.
- Keep the altered promise.

However, if the other person in the relationship does not agree to renegotiation, then you have two choices. You can do whatever is possible in order to keep the original promise. Or break it.

Breaking Your Promise

- To break a promise, communicate ahead of time.
- Speak precisely the promise you made.
- Tell the other person you will not be keeping the promise.
- Ask them to tell you the impact your broken promise creates.
- Apologize.
- Offer to make whatever restitution the other person thinks is appropriate.
- Make a *bigger* promise.

Communicating a broken promise after its due date creates a mess to be cleaned up. Clean it up anyway. Regain your honor.

Promises Made to Ourselves

We get down on ourselves when we do something we perceive as wrong, such as eating something not on our weight loss program. When this happens, have compassion for yourself. Ruthless compassion. Get rid of any wrongness. Instead, notice that your broken agreement occurred. Forgive yourself and remake your promise.

The Pitfalls of Promising

"Talk is not cheap. We cheapen talk."

We give our word too easily without being clear what it will take to keep it.

When you break a promise and you acknowledge you did so, spare the other person your reasons. If you speak your reasons, you will convince yourself your story is so reasonable it justified the breaking of the promise. This is a trap – it transfers *your* power to the reasons.

There is no power in *not* making promises. This is an inappropriate technique to avoid breaking promises. You will only be as powerful as the promises you make. Big people make big promises. You must make big promises if you want your vision to come forth in the world. Also, if you want your job to work, your relationship to work, your life to work.

Rather than holding a promise as an obligation, hold it as an opportunity to gain power.

Give others permission to hold you to account for any broken promises.

One sign of being out of integrity is that you experience yourself as small.

As you progress along the path of Elder, look for opportunities to clean up areas where you are out of integrity.

Life Areas to Examine for Out-Integrity

- Career
- Family/Relationships
- Finances
- Friendship
- Health and Well-being
- Home Environment
- Making a Difference
- Romance/Sex
- Security
- Self
- Spirituality
- Success
- Vacations/Hobbies
- Work Environment

Exercise #5: Integrity

Rate each of the life areas (and your relationship with each person inside each of these areas) on a scale of 1 to 10, with 10 being magnificent, over the top, flourishing. Those you rated lowest are where you have the most out-integrity.

This is where you have an *in*authentic relationship to your word. Holding this as a possibility, you can tell that truth to yourself, and tell that truth to the other. Doing so will bring yourself back into integrity.

Rate only the areas themselves. Do not allow the mind to rate You. You are not insufficient because of low ratings. Hold low ratings as an opportunity, not as an accusation, personal evaluation, or condemnation.

Consider this: If you find yourself reticent to speak with another, you are out of integrity with that person. If you find yourself avoiding the examination of one of the areas, you are out of integrity there.

Creating integrity in your life is particularly challenging in the present OR worldview. We live inside the OR agreement of cheap talk, where what passes for friendship is often little more than an acquaintanceship with this background agreement: *I won't call you on your stuff (lack of integrity) if you don't call me on mine.*

However, Elder steps out of this comfort zone, going beyond mere individuality into the realm of relationship-as-Self. Elder demands relationships be clean, demands they be in integrity. Not only does Elder demand this of the Self, but insists that others relate to her with integrity.

This is uncomfortable. The mind will whine, *"How can I demand this of another if my own integrity is out?"*

Your answer will be a correlate to love, compassion, and knowing the other as the Self. You can develop a deep appreciation that, in the courageous supporting of another to keep an agreement with you, *you are listening as well.* What you demand of the other, you must now demand of yourself.

How to Create Unworkability in Life

- Break a promise.
- Don't clean it up.
- As a result, you cannot listen to promises made *to* you.
- You become untrusting of others.
- You become angry.
- You become bitter.
- You die.
- No one comes to your funeral.
- Everyone who greets you when you pass over thinks this is funny and laughs at you, saying, *"It didn't need to be that hard, you know."*
- You sulk and have to come back to do it again.
- Next time, you smarten up and start the Path to Elder sooner.

The Seduction of Standards

Each of us has developed a set of principles we use to guide ourselves in life. As a generality, these are the same principles constituting Elder. They are what our soul knows. They are at the heart of being human. You will likely find your personal Principles and Values in the List of Attributes of Elder.

Standards of Comparison

We are not always present to our principles. This is because the mind is in the way.

Take the principle of generosity as an example. Our Essence is generous. The Self wants everyone to have enough of what really matters – love, kindness, and compassion.

The mind, however, has no interest in generosity or in anyone else having enough of, well, anything. The mind is stingy, wanting everything for itself. It has a "to hell with your Essence and to hell with everyone else" attitude. Remember that the untrained mind is interested in only one thing – its own survival. The mind's haven for survival is the past, so it wants us only to live only as we did in the past.

One method the mind has to keep us imprisoned in the past is by using a set of nasty tools – Standards of Comparison. I will refer to them simply as Standards. These are a judgmental aspect of the dichotomy, *better than/less than.* The mind uses standards to keep you in weakness and uncertainty.

It works this way: Let's say you decide to be generous with a monetary gift. The mind notices and hastens to abort this move on your part by starting a familiar pattern of thinking:

> *You don't have enough money to be generous ... he's got way more money than you do ... he doesn't care about you anyway ... don't be stupid enough to give him money....*

Should and Ought To

Standards are a set of weapons, but they are disguised. What makes them weapons is easier to observe if you add this phrase after each of the mind's statements: *"and it shouldn't be that way."*

Take the first of the mind's negative comments, for instance: *You don't have enough money to be generous.* Now add *"and it shouldn't be that way."* Notice both the standard and the ideal against which you do not match up.

The mind is really saying *you don't have enough money "and you should have."* You have been slammed by your own mind into uncertainty. Strike! Chalk one up for the mind.

Now go back and add *"and it shouldn't be that way"* to each objection the mind dredged up. See how your mind is using standards and ideals as weapons to keep You (Essence, Being, Self) off-balance, uncertain, and disempowered. You have been compared to an ideal and judged insufficient.

Your principle, generosity, was disempowered. Strike two! You are doing badly this time at bat.

How stupid you are being, and you "shouldn't be that way." Strike three! You're out! Game over! You have been slammed back into the past with the same old relationship with your friend you wanted to be generous with, and with the same old relationship with yourself. The mind wins again.

You can observe the standards game your mind plays by noticing when you think or say *should* or *ought to.* These are both red flags.

At first, you might find it easier to listen to others. You will hear both the standard and its ideal. For instance, yesterday I heard a woman in line at the market say, "They ought to have more lines open." The standard is clear – more lines. And the ideal is also implied – "Grocery stores ought to have enough cashiers at every moment so no one (me) has to wait in line."

Let's be clear, though. You have standards, everybody does. You always have and you always will. It is a human thing. Standards can be useful to measure your progress against. They only become an issue when the *standards use you.* And they only use you when you are unconscious of them.

Used with purpose, standards work wonderfully. This purposeful and aware use is not a function of the mind. Rather, it is a function of You, your Essence, your Being, for such use is aware.

Notice Your Standards

Remember, the name of the game is not to get rid of standards, nor to get rid of intolerance. It is about noticing. It is about observing. It is about becoming conscious of what you have been *un*conscious of. You will always have a mind and you will always have standards.

Five Distinctions to Complete the Past

The past must be completed. This is the task of the self-training of Elder. Thus far, I have outlined the roles of paradox and conflation and presented the bedrock role of integrity. There are five other distinctions:

- Forgiveness
- Apology
- Responsibility
- Compassion
- Listening

These five are distinct, but they are neither separate nor separable. Like fingers on a hand, they work together and are mutually interdependent. Each is necessary in order for all to be complete, to be whole, to have integrity.

Forgiveness

One critical aspect of cleaning up your past is to forgive those you believe have hurt you. To forgive means to give up resentment, to no longer wish the other harm, to no longer want to even the score, to no longer hold the other in blame. If the least of these remains, one has not yet fully forgiven. To be unforgiving is like attending a banquet, only to discover *you* are the main course.

There is a common saying: *Oh, I forgive. But I never forget!* Be wary, for this is also a common reason the mind uses to not forgive. Perhaps you can turn to this instead: *I have totally forgiven and mostly I have even forgotten.*

You will know you have forgiven when, happening upon a memory, it is accompanied by no emotion or merely amusement instead of negative emotions.

Forgiveness has nothing to do with the other person. It only has to do with you. Forgiveness lies outside our considerations about right and wrong. Rumi, the Sufi poet, speaks of forgiveness this way: "Beyond our ideas of right-doing and wrong-doing, there is a field. I'll meet you there."

Forgiveness is about freeing yourself from the automatic focus on your old perceived wrongs. Such focus takes too much of your energy. If you were to forgive everybody and everything *including yourself,* you could free yourself from the ropes of self-bondage.

This includes forgiving your parents whether living or dead, forgiving the person who did *something terrible* to you, and forgiving every single person you feel has hurt you. For some, this means forgiving God.

Exercise #6: Forgiveness

Ask yourself who you resent and who you feel negativity toward. Make a list of every name you think of even if you are not sure why. Trust the mind to bring the right names to the surface. It delights the mind to do this. Be specific. For example, instead of writing "my mother," write her full name.

Just as basketball cannot be played in the stands, a written exercise cannot be done only in the mind. Reality rules on paper. Write the list.

Once you have your list, become present to what happened with each person. Write down what you recall about each one.

Note: Do not read further until your list is finished. The mind will want to keep reading this page. Don't do it. Do the writing first.

* * * * *

Before proceeding further, consider this as a possibility: *there is nothing to forgive.*

Here's what I mean. People do what they do because the situation shows up for them a certain way. In his book, *The Three Laws of Performance: Rewriting the Future of Your Organization and Your Life,* Steve Zaffron says that this is the primary law about human behavior: **"How people perform correlates to how situations occur to them."**

It tells us that, though you might not know why they did what they did (performed that way), you would know why they did it *if you knew how the situation occurred to them.* You would not only know it, it *would make sense.*

Most actions are automatic and designed to be in one's own best interest. Other people's actions *have nothing to do with you.* That you feel hurt by an action (including a speech action) can happen. But that's *you* feeling hurt, not them hurting you. Big difference.

Consider the possibility that it is self-centered to believe another person's actions were any more personal than the rain. The rain may get you wet, certainly, but it wasn't aimed at you. You just happened to be in the way of the raindrops as they headed to the ground. In short, what the rain did *wasn't about you.*

One time I attended a seminar. I was seated in a large group in which a woman spoke emotionally about the sexual abuse she suffered as a young child at the hands of her uncle. Many of us were moved to tears. When she finished speaking, she was still caught up in the anger of her memories.

The leader waited a moment, then quietly asked, "Do you suppose your uncle would have treated you any differently *if you had been anyone else but you?*"

The woman was puzzled at first. "Well, no. I don't think so."

The leader said, "Then why are you taking it personally?"

The room was silent. The woman gasped, then started to laugh. She laughed until she dissolved into tears. Possibly tears of relief, because they were mixed with laughter.

She had, of course, taken the abuse personally. I realized that I too had taken personally many incidents that had not been personally directed at me. They had been the other person's issue, not mine.

This perspective had never occurred to me before. Suddenly, just by listening to that exchange, that baggage, no longer personal, just fell away.

Not Personal

The whole concept of forgiveness is based on the mistaken idea that the action was personal, aimed at you, and intended to cause you pain. If you realize people simply *do what they do,* and what happens to us is simply *what happens to us,* then we can take *nothing* personally. With such a shift in view, nothing needs to be forgiven and no one needs to be forgiven, including ourselves.

While this is accurate, the mind does not want to believe it. Regardless of the mind's objection, however, it works to forgive everybody and everything. Forgiveness is neither *for* the other person nor *about* the other. Rather, it is for *you*.

Forgiveness results in freedom – *your* freedom.

Forgiveness is a distinction, yet it is inseparable from conflation and from responsibility. You can create a more powerful and useful story. Once you see your role as *the teller of your story,* you might consider that you are a hundred percent responsible – not for the facts, but for what you say the facts meant – the story.

Elders take the stand that they are *totally responsible* for how their life has turned out. When you take that stand, forgiveness is easy.

If you are not willing to take the responsibility, you are stuck with a continual focus on and imprisonment by your mind's commitment that *you are right and they are wrong.* This is the prison of the past.

Now, having said there is "nothing to forgive," nonetheless forgiveness is an active action, deliberately taken. To speak "I forgive" is a powerful declarative act, in the same realm as the umpire declaring that a pitch is a ball or a strike.

He can do this because he has been empowered to make that declaration. His is not merely an assertion, a matter of fact or evidence. It is a declaration and his speaking makes it so. A wise Elder umpire said this, "Some are balls and some are strikes. But they are *nothing* until I call them."

It is like that with forgiveness. You, source of your life, are empowered to declare "I forgive." It is a declarative act. So declare yourself forgiven. Declare others forgiven. Take down the damn bars of your prison! What you give up is your sense of entitlement, your righteousness. What you gain is your life. Choose.

Apology

You might want to call or visit each person on your negative feelings list. Tell each person you take full responsibility in the matter.

While it is common to say I *forgive you for x,* this does not work because the other person bristles at the idea they did anything they need to be forgiven for. Nor does it work to say *I am sorry for x,* or *I am sorry that....*

This is not straight talk.

Instead, it is better to say, *I apologize* or *I apologize for holding you responsible.* Do not give them explanations or reasons for your thinking or behavior. Doing so is your mind justifying your actions in an effort to stay "right." Don't do it. Just apologize. Apologizing will free you. It is such a magnanimous act, so *beyond* our ideas of *right*-doing and *wrong*-doing.

This takes courage, particularly the first time. It gets easier with each person you talk to from your list. After all, do you *really* want the debilitating energy of non-forgiveness in your life?

On Forgiving Yourself

People travel this lifetime with low-level grudges against themselves. You can hear it when they talk. They put themselves down; they seem to feel inadequate, perhaps even thinking they don't deserve to be on the planet. You know them. These are your friends and neighbors, maybe your relatives. Possibly you.

Yet we are all good enough. We might even say that each of us is perfect exactly the way we are and exactly the way we are not. Isn't it bizarre that we have an entire population staying apart from each other because each member feels they are not good enough? We accuse ourselves, we try ourselves, we convict ourselves, we judge ourselves, and we sentence ourselves to a lifetime in prison. A prison we build for ourselves.

What arrogance to believe we have the right to beat ourselves up like that! Instead, we all need to forgive ourselves for all that human stuff, those imagined transgressions, those imagined inadequacies. Remember who you are – a spiritual being on a human journey within a bizarre You OR Me world. You are doing the best you can within the limits of the culture. So give yourself a break.

There is no forgiveness needed. And forgive yourself anyway.

You might wish to stand in front of a mirror and say "I forgive you and I love you." Say this out loud, and say it as many times as you need to until you and the one in the mirror get it. Keep on repeating this phrase for as long as you feel emotional.

You can stop when one of you says, "Yeah, yeah, yeah; enough already."

Responsibility

We tend to conflate facts with story. We also tend to conflate responsibility with fault and blame.

Remember the story of being struck by the bus? If that had happened to you, there are two questions you might ask. The first is the automatic question: *Why did that bus hit me?*

This is the easy question, for you can make up all sorts of reasons. It is also not worth asking because inanimate objects don't *have* reasons. The question implies that you are the victim – poor you, the bus did it *to* you. This question lies within the realm of fault and blame. It is neither responsible nor useful.

However, there is a second question you might ask. One that might provide useful answers. *What was I doing in the space the bus was about to go through?*

This is a useful question. Asking it opens something useful, that is, the *possibility of responsibility.*

The Possibility of Being Responsible for Your Life

Any answer you give to the second question will be made up. It will come out of your imagination. But it will lead to the possibility of taking responsibility for what happened. This is useful because it engages your imagination. Taking responsibility does not mean the situation that occurred was your fault. There is no fault or blame in responsibility.

A simple way to define responsibility is this: responsibility is the *willingness* to take the stand that you are *cause in the matter.*

Take a closer look at this by examining some answers we could make up to the question, *What was I doing in the space the bus was about to go through?*

1. Well, I was there. I was the one standing in that space.

2. I had always wanted to feel what it was like to be struck, lightly, by a bus.

3. The bus driver looked like my ex-brother-in-law and I never liked him so I willed him to hit me so I could get even with him later.

Ridiculous? No, imaginative. Such a question has a double value. Imaginative answers take us out of automatic victimhood *and* constitute a valuable way to practice taking responsibility for what has happened to us in life.

Elders take the stand that we are each responsible for our own lives. Though taking responsibility is important for an Adult to be effective, Elder takes it further. Elders take responsibility for what and whom they put themselves around. Elders take responsibility for what comes out of their mouth, and they take responsibility for their experience of life.

React or Respond

There is a magnificent section in a book I was given as a third year medical student. Originally entitled *From Death Camp to Existentialism,* Victor Frankl's book was later retitled, *Man's Quest for Meaning.*

A Jewish psychiatrist, Frankl had been incarcerated in a concentration camp during World War II. His wife and most of his relatives were murdered. In the book, he tells of a realization that "made me freer than the guards."

Frankl noticed that between a stimulus and the reaction, there is always a moment when one can *respond* rather than react. This observation points to our basic human design. We are not automatic reaction machines. We are not designed to flutter and bob to every circumstantial wind. Rather we are powerful beings able to *choose our responses.*

Choice is powerful. We can exercise our free will to select a response freely. We can choose to forgive, we can choose to apologize, we can choose to declare ourselves magnificent. And we can choose to take responsibility rather than assign it to something outside ourselves. We can choose to declare that we are *responsible* for our actions, our attitudes, our points of view, and our moods.

Further, we can choose *what is so to be what is so.* Life is so much easier when we stop resisting what is so and choose to see what *is so* as being the *way it is.*

Responsibility is not fault, blame, or guilt. It is as simple and clear as President Harry Truman's famous quote, "The buck stops here."

After all, if it is not you who is responsible for your life, who might it be? Have you ever seen an advertisement offering, "I will be responsible for your life. Bargain sale this week only"? Most teenagers at one point or another say to their parents, "Hey, I didn't ask to be born!" The wise mother might reply, "Really? You quite sure about that?"

Victimhood as a Mind Game

> *"Most men live lives of quiet desperation and go to the grave with their song still in them."* – Henry David Thoreau

It is irresponsible to claim we are products of outside forces. This is the opposite of taking responsibility. This is the speaking of the mind. When we abdicate responsibility for our own experience of life, we turn our lives over to some outside force.

Perhaps we have assigned our life (either the credit or the fault or the blame) to parents, to a spouse, to a boss or to some other authority. We might even try to make "the times" responsible for our lives.

Life just doesn't work that way. To have a great life, we must take the stand that each of us are sovereign beings. Regardless of whether we have been brought up within the arms of Mary or put out upon the windy cliff to shift for ourselves, we are each responsible for having our lives turn out.

Adult tends to live inside a world of victim mentality. This victim mentality takes many forms, the most prominent being cynicism and resignation. Cynicism is a way of saying *all is bad and will always be.* Resignation is similar: *Oh well, things are (sigh) just the way they are.* Both are irresponsible. Both are realms of suffering wherein others (people or circumstances) have been granted inappropriate power.

The victim mentality can be subtle. We can observe it in the choice of words spoken by those who are *against* things, and those who rely on terms like *injustice, wrongfulness,* and *those poor people.* Such speakers consider themselves to be underdogs and feel oppressed by governments, trends, societies. They believe in conspiracy theories.

Remember that Elders have minds that include *everything we are attributing to Adult.* The victim mentality does not disappear in the Elder stage. It is still present, but it can be held differently. It shifts from context to content. Elder owns it. Adult is owned *by* it.

Whining

To discover where you are NOT taking responsibility, listen to yourself when you whine.

To whine means to have a chronic complaint about the way something or someone shows up for you. *"And shouldn't be that way."* Further, you have a particular *way of being* associated with the complaint.

Whining begins with an ongoing, persistent, internal conversation of the mind put on loudspeaker. Whining is one of the techniques the mind uses to make itself right and others wrong. It is a form of irresponsibility, for the basis of whining is victimization.

Whining is a conversation that usually has its origin in early Youth. In order to root out your own whining, commit yourself to discover it, own it, and be the context for it. To have this happen quickly, enroll a trusted friend to point out when you whine.

All whining follows a particular pattern. Whining has both a payoff and a cost – a payoff for the mind and a cost to You. The payoff for the mind is that it gets to be right and have the other be wrong. This is one of the favorite tools of the mind.

The cost of whining is a loss of affinity with others. This loss of affinity decreases your aliveness and enthusiasm for life. This results in a loss of vitality, self-expression, and the sense that your world is safe. This is a high cost indeed. It diminishes You.

(See Notes.)

Sarcasm

Consider sarcasm as saying the opposite of what you mean. Sarcasm is a form of irresponsibility.

Sarcasm keeps you a victim. It is also designed to confuse the listener, now burdened with the task of trying to figure out if you mean what you said or its opposite.

Sarcasm functions to shut down communication. It is a form of withdrawal, substituting for straight talk. It is a form of manipulation, another of the mind's games.

Straight Talk

Straight talk matters. Straight talk is saying what you mean and meaning what you say. Neither whining nor sarcasm are straight talk.

As Elders train themselves, whining and sarcasm both fall away. These are replaced in the course of life itself with integrity, responsibility, forgiveness, and straight talk.

Compassion and Love

"Two things stand like stone. Kindness in another's troubles. Courage in your own." – Adam Lindsey Gordon

We cannot speak of compassion without speaking of love first. Not romantic love, but love from the larger perspective.

Consider the possibility that love is not limited to a human condition, but that its meaning is vast, even cosmic. There is a power, a force that has the universe be the way it is, the force containing all the laws. Many call that God. Others call it G.O.D. the Grand Organizing Design. Both terms point to the *glue holding it all together.* When I refer to love, I mean that glue.

Love is *acceptance,* which means to acknowledge the legitimate presence of something. So to love you means to accept you the way you are and the way you are not. This is human love.

Love is also present in the tree root accepting the presence of the dirt, and the dirt accepting the presence of the tree root. And in the moon accepting the presence of the sun.

Love, the acceptance of the other, is like a profound endorsement – an endorsement of the legitimate existence of the other. Moreover, if were to speak of love at the most powerful level of unity, there is, of course, no "other."

The Meaning of Compassion

This story was told by Andrew Harvey in his book, *The Hope: A Guide to Sacred Activism*:

"I interviewed his Holiness (the Dalai Lama) for *Elle Magazine.* At the end of our hour together, spent in his small, bare hotel room, I stood up, plucked up my courage, and asked him, *What is the meaning of life?*

"His Holiness flung back his head, and roared with laughter. Then he grew intensely concentrated and still.

"*The meaning of life,* he said quietly, leaning forward to touch my forehead with his, *is to embody compassion. Anyone can discover this. When you discover this and live it, you discover your truest nature and share its joy."*

Compassion as an aspect of love means the willingness to be present with and endorse the reality and legitimacy of the suffering of another. The Dalai Lama also says that love and compassion are necessities, not luxuries. Without them, he says, humanity cannot survive.

Roshi Joan Halifax says that it is inherent in being human that we aspire to transform another's suffering. She points out that in Buddhism compassion requires "a strong back and a soft front."

This means having the equanimity to stand with courage in the face of our own adversity, to accept that circumstances are the way they are and not some other way. It also means to take responsibility, to accept that you participated in their creation. A strong back.

To have a soft front means to face the world with an undefended heart. This is exhibited by Quan Yin, a female archetype who perceives the cries of suffering in the world. For thousands of years, women, particularly crones, have exemplified Quan Yin's acceptance of suffering as it is, bringing to it the strength of compassion, and thus infusing societies with kindness.

Randy McNamara, senior Landmark Forum leader, says that having compassion in daily life includes knowing what another must give up in order to grant your request. Thich Nhat Hanh writes eloquently of compassion in the book *Love Is Compassion in Action.*

You might want to do some reading on the subject yourself as you examine what it means for an Elder to embody love and compassion.

The Myth of *Stop It!*

Handling issues from the past does not mean stopping them. You cannot have something stop by stopping it. Stopping is a result, not an action. And it is a result you must address indirectly because it lives within the paradox of *you can't get there from here.*

Something will stop naturally when you disappear the condition(s) holding it in place. This is one result of the basic law of how human beings work: *Re-creation Causes Disappearance.*

As an example, when you notice that you are whining, your first urge will be to stop it. Not a good idea. If you stop, you abort the opportunity to notice your whining in all its force and glory. Much better to deliberately whine louder and longer. This shifts whining from the context-that-has-you (your mind) to You as context for your whining as a piece of content.

To whine at effect is merely to be an ongoing whiner. To whine at cause is mastery. When Elders whine, they whine at cause. And whining at cause can be hilarious.

The Myth of Being a Good Person

One of the myths of our culture (using myth in the sense of a superstition) is that we can become good human beings. Labeling this belief a myth seems strange because isn't this what most people are trying to do? Become the best human being we can?

The reality is that we are perfect just as we are. The key to this as a myth resides in the word *becoming*. Trying to *become* a good human being is like trying to have arms. Somewhat foolish, given we already have arms.

A Sufi Parable

A Sufi teaching tells of the man who visited a great mystic to find out how to let go of his chains of attachment and his prejudices. Instead of answering him directly, the mystic jumped to his feet and bolted to a nearby pillar. He flung his arms around it, grasping the marble surface as he screamed, "Save me from this pillar! Save me from this pillar."

The man who had asked the question could not believe what he saw. He thought the mystic was mad. The shouting soon brought a crowd of people.

"Why are you doing that?" the man asked. "I came to you to ask a spiritual question because I thought you were wise, but obviously you are crazy. You are holding the pillar; the pillar is not holding you. You can simply let go."

The mystic let go of the pillar and said to the man, "If you can understand that, you have your answer. Your chains of attachment are not holding you, you are holding them. You can simply let go."

* * * * *

Consider the possibility that each of us is perfect just the way we are, and that we have barriers to the experience and expression of that perfection. We don't have to work to become *good* or *better* or *perfect,* for we already are all those things. This is our Being, our Essence.

What Elders work on are the *barriers* to that perfection. They work on the barriers listed as Traits of the Mind.

Listening: Communication That Works

Elders focus on living within the realm of Being. In this realm you have a powerful tool: communication.

You live in the world with others. Your presence communicates with them; your posture communicates as well. Who you are, what you say, and what you do not say form your communication with others.

A widespread view is that communication occurs whenever a speaker broadcasts a verbal piece of information to a listener. This is akin to throwing a ball with accuracy.

However, there is a more powerful view. We can observe that communication has not occurred in such an instance. Instead, communication only occurs when a listener has perceived the information *in the same manner the speaker intended.*

The first view claims communication is a function of the clarity of the speaking. This means when a speaker speaks clearly, this is sufficient. The job is done and the speaker is not responsible for more.

This is not the Elder's view of communication.

Listening Is the Key

The second view focuses on the critical importance of the listener. What the speaker said is *rarely what is heard.* And what is heard is what matters.

We each have a personal set of filters through which every communication must pass. We let some words through, but not others. We let some meanings through, but not others. We let some speech tones through, but not others. It is automatic and unconscious.

Usually, both speaker and listener are unaware of these filters. The speaker assumes the listener has heard what was meant. The listener assumes she heard what the speaker both said and meant. Neither is accurate.

These filters mean that the *listener* is the key to effective communication, not the speaker. Effective communication focuses on the listeners identifying and owning their own filters through which information must pass. These filters, unnoticed, serve as powerful barriers to communication.

The Elder-in-training focuses on listening, but with an increasing awareness of the degree to which her filters alter what she hears.

After all, of what use is the bearded prophet on the street corner bellowing "The end is near!" if no one is listening? The first view of communication says he has communicated. Yet, he clearly has not if the passersby have filtered out his message.

The key to effective communication is to be an effective listener. Another way to say this is: *We do not speak something into existence. Rather we* listen *it into existence.*

Elder's task, then, is to listen Elder into existence. You see, both Youth and Adult would yearn to become Elder if they knew what that meant. Oddly enough, they actually do know.

The challenge for Elder is to realize that such a primal level of knowing has been covered over by mounting generations of time and disuse. The challenge for Elder is to give Adult (and Youth) the space and permission to discover this inner knowledge for themselves.

Elders can neither demand nor require that another step onto the Path of Elder. But if we give them the space, some will discover that internal knowing and yearning. Wisdom cannot be transmitted; wisdom must be discovered. *Elders facilitate the self-discovery of wisdom of the Self.* And they facilitate that by listening powerfully.

The Art of Broken Silence

When you stand back and observe yourself and others, you will notice that people are often silent. We actually speak a rather small percentage of the time. Even when we are with others, our *natural* state is silence.

Even so, most people tend to talk a lot, often filling every niche with words. Why? Personally, I feel anxious when I sit across from someone and the two of us just look at one another, not speaking. My mind says I need to speak of something, anything, to break the awkward silence. The mind craves the familiar and chatter is familiar, not silence.

Yet, when two Beings are profoundly together, silence is natural. To facilitate that, you might want to ask yourself if there is a reason to speak, to break the silence. You may ask yourself the larger question: Is there an Art of Broken Silence? Perhaps wisdom has a greater opportunity to arise in the Unbroken Silence.

I am not suggesting that to listen means not to speak. That would be like asking the bird not to sing. Rather, the opportunity is to notice how much we speak as though on automatic pilot.

Powerful Listening Techniques

There are listening techniques that allow the mind's filters to be present but NOT block. The most effective way is to be an active listener. This means to actually listen rather than plan what you will say next. Active listening allows you to give the speaker feedback before the mind distorts the speaker's words to its liking.

Your feedback can be of two types. The simplest way is to repeat the words back to the speaker. (It works best to preface the conversation by informing the other person you will be doing this.)

For example, "What I heard you say was you have never seen a pig fly. Did I hear you correctly*?"* The speaker is often delighted someone actually heard what was said. This is a gift to the speaker. It also slows the conversation down to a human pace.

The second technique is to paraphrase after a few sentences. This has almost the same positive effect – warmth, understanding, and the pleasure of knowing one was heard. It also slows the conversation less than verbatim feedback. "What I heard you say is you are really unhappy with your job, and your boss is incompetent, and you are frightened you might be fired. Did I get that right?"

Equally important is the effect on you. You have done the work, you have served the speaker. And it is indeed work to listen to another like this. It takes focus, a quiet mind, and a commitment to another's well-being and growth. This is compassion. And this is love in action. This is Elder.

One lovely result of a compassionate conversation is the quiet satisfaction of being *with* another human being. The built-in separation of our OR worldview vanishes for those moments. And one of these moments tends to lead to other moments of what could be called joy and love and belonging, the we-ness that is our human birthright. This we-ness is known as *resonance.*

Listening Gives and Receives

Elder Training is dependent upon practicing this kind of listening. And active listening both gives and receives. By re-creating their speaking, you allow others to hear themselves. In addition, you are training yourself. It only takes one other person to be able to practice.

As the old joke goes:

> *A visitor to New York is lost. She asks a passerby, "Can you tell me how to get to Carnegie Hall?"*
>
> *The person answers, "Sure. Practice, practice, practice."*

How do you best get Elder Training? Listen, listen, listen.

How do you best train Elders? Listen, listen, listen.

Learning Occurs Best in a Group

> *"When two or more are gathered in my name, I shall be there."* – Jesus of Nazareth

When two or more are gathered for the purpose of serving mankind by becoming Elders, Spirit (Being) shall be there too. Even though you have the ultimate responsibility of training yourself, it is not a solitary task. You don't have to do it alone.

Self-training lives best inside the context of a group. The group may be as little as two people, with you as student and another as teacher.

Within a single individual, the mind tends to overpower the Self. However, when two or more individuals gather together, two Selves are capable of overcoming the mind. Thus the necessity for another, ideally a teacher who is a fellow traveler on the path to Elder.

While it might be advantageous to have a teacher who has been on the Elder trail a bit longer than you, it is not essential. The "teachership" in a cohort of two will shift from one to the other.

The larger the group on the path together, the stronger the presence of Being-ness. The strong Being-ness of a group will function more effectively to keep the mind where it belongs, as servant. In such a group, mind-as-servant will allow itself to be trained, for it will feel safe.

Remember that the purpose of the mind is to cause the survival of the Being. When the mind gets frightened, it will rebel. It is less likely to rebel in a group with much Being-ness.

Characteristics of an Elder Training Group

Elder training within a group tends to be both broader and deeper than self-training. The phenomenon of group creates an ambience for rapid learning. In addition, a group develops a resonance and an identity over time, and this becomes larger than the individual's identity.

As you become more identified with a group, your identity will expand from Self-as-individual to Self-as-group. This is a stepping stone on the way to the ultimate identity of Self-as-humanity and Self-as-Spirit.

Find a group within which you feel comfortable. Trust your intuition for you will know when you feel at home in a group. However, do not confuse this with the mind's intention for you to stay with the familiar, the comfortable, the past. It is better not to feel too much at home.

Form a Group

You might choose to create a group yourself. You may start with a group of two. To form a larger group, you can enroll members from other groups of intentional people. In every community, no matter how small, there are groups committed to doing good. These can be church groups, PTAs, book clubs, meet-ups, and the like.

Another method is to gather a group of people from your friends and acquaintances. Share with them your interest in training yourself to become an Elder. Ask them whether they have a similar interest.

You could also build a discussion group to focus on this book. Or on other books.

It will become clear who in your group has interest and commitment. Some people will leave and some will stay. Work with those who stay.

You don't have to convince anybody that becoming Elder is the *right* thing to do. Joining puts a person on the Path to Elder, whether or not they remain in the group.

Be prepared for the group to change and shift over time, just as family did, yet more quickly.

What Constitutes a "Group That Works?"

Groups vary in quality. Most groups in our competitive culture are made up of competitive members. Each member has a mind that is alert, wary, and quick to make itself right and all other members wrong. Being in a group brings up past history, activating old wounds and defenses.

While these are all useful challenges to be worked with, it requires a certain deftness and compassion. The mind frightens easily. If you scare the mind, you damage the group. A critical and primary function of any group is to create safety for the mind.

The Vistar Method

An effective technique for group management was developed by Ron and Victoria Friedman. The Vistar Method is the one I resonate with the most.

I compared the Vistar Method with the techniques of more than fifty group settings over a period of nearly forty years, in addition to hundreds of college and medical school courses and medical meetings. The Vistar Method seems to work best.

It results in an openness and a depth of speaking and listening because it endorses the validity of each speaker. The technique allows group members to focus on what the speaker is saying rather than the mind's agreeing, disagreeing, or rehearsing. Further, it allows the development of a *groupness* which has been referred to as "resonance at the soul level."

While one can be trained in the Vistar Method (check them out at www.VistarFoundation.org), their guide rules are not exclusive. Vistar utilizes the same underlying guide rules that allow any group to function effectively, whether indigenous groups coming into alignment around the evening fire, a teacher maintaining order in a first grade classroom or the decision-making of a corporate board of directors.

- Raise your hand to contribute. Wait to be called on.
- Speak to the topic; contributions are from one to three minutes.
- No questions during the circle.
- No cross-talk.

A Few Words About Group

We are not used to being in groups that work. Our *You OR Me* worldview causes them to NOT work. Allow me to point out a few things you might find useful to assist a group to function well.

Just as an Elder takes one hundred percent responsibility for the quality of his/her relationships, so too an Elder takes responsibility for the effectiveness, structure, and function of the group as a whole. Just as the self-training of an Elder requires discipline and commitment, so too an effective group requires the same.

The group meeting is, to use the analogy of American football, the huddle between plays. The action takes place on the field between huddles. Thus, homework is critical.

The purpose of the group is twofold: to serve as a container for the self-training of its members; and to function as a springboard for each member to source other groups.

Be aware that groups devolve. *Groups tend to devolve in size.* Members move away, develop other interests, or die. For the group to continue to be effective, recruitment of new members must be built in.

Groups tend to devolve in quality. Without care, groups devolve to become groups of mere *being-ness* without action. They can become social groups or psychological support groups unless a constant reminder is built in to maintain purpose.

Groups need structure and rules, and the rules need to be written. Structure needs to be strong enough to provide a container of effectiveness, and gentle enough to provide a container of safety.

Elders in Training have access to three venues of self-training:

- one-on-one
- within a group
- within the family group

While these are distinct, they have a common denominator. The training is one-on-one. All trainings come down to this. Even when a group has a thousand people, the critical core is one-on-one because each individual committed to self-development will hear others speaking as though *just to me.*

The Role of the Family

For hundreds of thousands of years, Elders developed within family and tribe. For eons, family consisted of three generations living together: children, parents, and grandparents. Each generation trained the generations arising.

Thus, the training of Elders was accomplished naturally by grandparents, parents, peers, and later by their own children and, eventually, their grandchildren. Elders received a five-generation training.

Today, the family has fragmented to the point that most Elders are trained only by their parents, if at all. I wish I could add that we get trained by our children, but this is not often the case. Children today are too busy, too wired-in. By the time Adult becomes an age appropriate to enter Elderhood, they arrive virtually untrained.

The inherent and time-honored role of a grandparent is to function as Elder for the benefit of the family. The primary function of Elder has not changed because family structure has temporarily detoured.

As an Elder-in-training, one of your tasks is to function as Elder for your family, regardless of distance, time, or agreement. After all, Elder is about service, not about power or recognition. One can serve from afar. Proximity, though desirable, is not a requirement for Elder.

Once you commit to serving as Elder within your family of origin, they will train you. This training might show up as resistance to what you have to offer.

This is an opportunity for any lack of integrity to show up and be handled. Clean up the mess. Not only the mess you have made, but the mess made by the culture with you as its agent.

You may discover you have no authority in your family. It is not unusual for Elder to find they cannot make anything happen. This does not mean you are without influence.

As an Elder, you will find what is needed in the family and provide it. As an Elder, you will have much influence indeed.

The Revitalized Role of Elder

One longstanding role of Elder was the bringer of outside information. No longer.

In 1977, Buckminster Fuller, world visionary and architect of the geodesic dome, described one of Elder's loss points during an interview with Werner Erhard.

"Early, Mom and Dad were, for their children, the authority regarding their lives. Dad ranged wide during his search for food, staying aware of any possible dangers arriving from a distance. He brought home the meat.

"Mom consolidated these gains and developed the means to preserve the food, drying it, heating it with fire, and the like.... Both Mom and Dad were the [bringers of and] repository of the knowledge that allowed continued existence.

"This knowledge was confined to them and they were the exclusive conduit by which it passed [from their own parents] down to their children.

"One day as Dad came home, his children ran out to greet him and they told him the radio said someone had flown across the Atlantic.

"*What!?* Dad exclaimed.

"Dad never again brought home some news."

From then on, outside news came from elsewhere. This was a loss point, a devolutionary down-step.

But bringing in outside information was only one of the roles Elder played, a relatively minor one. It only appears important when seen through the distorted lens of Adult's worship of the *Breaking News!*

In our present global community, news is conveyed electronically, the Internet and countless television stations overwhelming our minds with information. We are drowning in knowledge while starving for wisdom.

Elder as Bringer of Inside Information: Wisdom

The Roles of Elder were much more important than mere "outside-news-bringer." This is still true.

To begin with, Elders are *risk-takers.* Why would they not be, after conquering fear and shame and the pull of the past? And knowing who they are at the core? And not having anything *important* to risk? Why would you *not* be a risk-taker?

> *"Security is mostly a superstition. It does not exist in nature, nor do the children of men as a whole experience it. Avoiding danger is no safer in the long run than outright exposure.*
>
> *"Life is either a daring adventure or nothing."* – Helen Keller

The risk-taking Elder can express at various levels: individual, relationship, family, group, nation, or world. Maggie Kuhn, a powerful social activist in the 1970s and '80s, examined the roles Elderhood can play at the cultural level. She suggests the main role of Elderhood is to heal and humanize society. Kuhn has pointed to specific ways Elder can make a difference:

- Mentoring the young, bringing them inside information, (e.g., what can be found in this book).
- Serving as family and cultural historians.
- Mediating conflict – civil, racial, or intergenerational.
- Serving as watchdog over the proper service of governmental agencies.
- Organizing causes and mobilizing social change.
- Leading the move away from adult self-interest toward the interests of all.
- Speaking and writing their vision for the future.

I have focused upon the former role of Elder as bringer of *outside* information, pointing out its relative lack of importance now, so as to contrast it to its more valuable role as the bringer of *inside* information.

This is what is missing in this bizarre culture of OR. Your work in the DKDK realm gives your words both relevance and authority. Elders step into that power.

> *"When you keep saying it the way it is, eventually your word becomes law in the universe."* – Werner Erhard

Where Do You Choose to Work?

The future of the beehive does not depend upon the action of a single bee, but upon the activity of the hive as a whole. In this same way, you alone cannot impact the culture directly. Individuals do not interact *directly* with culture, but indirectly through group and institution.

Nonetheless, with others, you can co-create with others a future for humanity.

> *"We are the first species on this Earth who is conscious of evolution, conscious we are affecting our own evolution by everything we do, conscious ultimately that we are evolution becoming self-aware.*
>
> *"Evolution by chance is becoming evolution by choice."* – Barbara Marx Hubbard

Choices

As an Elder, you have the power to transform lives by your actions. You can transform lives by both the creativity of your speaking and the space-creation of your listening. This is true regardless whether or not you are in a position of authority.

> *"Elders legitimize, endorse and underscore the value of the younger."* – Anonymous

You may have already done extensive work at the basic level of individual. In your Essence, you are aware you did the work so you could make a difference in the lives of others.

At what level do you choose to make that difference? No level is more important than another. How much leverage are you willing to take on? It is your choice and there is no right answer.

You might wish to work at the level of relationship (one-on-one), at the level of group (family or other), at the level of organization, or at the level of institution (education, economics, finance, government).

Perhaps you will choose to work at the level of nation or at the level of humanity.

You might discover it doesn't matter which level *you* choose. Instead, you may discover that the level chooses you. Nor is it important to *actively* choose, for choice will work within you and you might discover you have *already* chosen.

Choice is not always a personal phenomenon. By consistently saying YES to whatever shows up in front of you and doing the work to complete your past, you create sufficient open space that, by the Law of Attraction, you draw to yourself that which is perfect for you.

You can allow *something-there-is-that-guides-my-life-and-looks-not-like-me* to work through you. You can title it whatever you wish: God, Spirit, intuition, Providence, love, or just a good hunch. The name matters little. It is more a matter of getting the mind out of the way of *that-which-wants-to-give-birth-through-you.*

In short, you can simply go for it! After all, the bottom line is this: service is service. And Elders serve.

Service

Ron Pevny, Director of the Center for Conscious Eldering and Author, *Conscious Living, Conscious Aging,* says this about service:

"Service to others as a conscious elder is not defined by how big or visible our actions are. Rather, it is defined by the consciousness and love we bring to whatever we feel the need to do.

"Whether it is volunteer work, working for an income, an avocation, social activism, grandparenting, or spending special time serving as mentor to a young person, the form of how we serve others is not nearly as important as the intention, wholeness and self-awareness behind it.

"Conscious elderhood is about doing our best to serve with love in whatever circumstance we find ourselves while also honoring our need to deepen our inner lives and savor those precious days of life's elder chapters. The key is finding the balance that is right for us."

When you find yourself uncertain, either afraid to take the next step or not knowing how, consider this poem by David Whyte:

Start Close In

by David Whyte

Start close in, don't take the second step
or the third,
start with the first thing close in,
the step you don't want to take.

Start with the ground you know,
the pale ground beneath your feet,
your own way of starting the conversation.

Start with your own question,
give up on other people's questions,
don't let them smother something simple.

To find another's voice,
follow your own voice,
wait until that voice becomes a
private ear listening to another.

Start right now, take a small step
you can call your own
don't follow someone else's
heroics, be humble and focused,
start close in, don't mistake
that other for your own.

*Start close in, don't take
the second step or the third,
start with the first thing
close in, the step
you don't want to take.*

Final Words

We are coming to the end of this Story, this learning tool, this instruction manual. You left home in search of that which demanded of you to be searched for. Following much hard work, you have discovered what you have been looking for – which turns out to be within rather than without.

Now you can see yourself rightly. Your Self was right in front of you all along. You were never really lost.

This is the end of my Story. You may choose it as your Story. Maybe you will choose to modify it to fit your belief system. As co-creator of humanity's evolution, you are free to evaluate the facts and create whatever Story supports your path. After all, it is your life and you create the Story of your life.

Welcome to the world of Elder. Welcome to a life of joy, freedom, enthusiasm, and contribution. Welcome to the world of You AND Me.

If you like, we can have a dialogue. My e-mail address is HarveyWAustin@yahoo.com. I will read what you write to me and I will allow it to sink in. I will acknowledge that I have read it. Perhaps we will speak to one another.

Harvey W. Austin, MD

www.HarveyWAustin.com
www.HarveyWAustin.wordpress.com
www.EldersRock.com

Notes

The materials entitled, "The Purpose of the Mind," are derived from The *est* Training, copyright Landmark Worldwide, LLC.

The distinction, "Recreation Causes Disappearance," is taken from The *est* Training, copyright Landmark Worldwide, LLC.

The terms "chronic complaint," "way of being associated with that complaint," "payoff," "costs" and "techniques the mind uses to make itself right and others wrong" are subsets of the distinction "Racket," as used in *The Three Laws of Performance,* by Steve Zaffron and Dave Logan, copyright 1994 Zaffron and Logan (Jossey-Bass, 1994), pp. 145-147.

A Global Response to Elder Abuse and Neglect: Building Primary Health Care Capacity to Deal with the Problem Worldwide: Main Report W.H.O. 2008 http://apps.who.int/iris/bitstream/10665/43869/1/9789241563581_eng.pdf

Jensen, Michael. *Integrity: Without it Nothing Works.* http://papers.ssrn.com/sol3/papers.cfm?abstract_id=1511274

Social Science Electronic Publishing (SSEP), Inc.; Harvard Business School; National Bureau of Economic Research (NBER); European Corporate Governance Institute (ECGI).

Reading List

1. Bach Richard. *Jonathan Livingston Seagull*, The Complete Edition, including Part Four. Scribner, 1970/2014.

2. Baker, Carolyn. *Collapsing Consciously: Transformative Truths for Turbulent Times* (Sacred Activism). North Atlantic Book, 2011.

3. Cooper, Dr. Marc Cooper and Selman, James C. *The Elder.* Sahalie Press, 2011.

4. Covey, Stephen R. *The 7 Habits of Highly Effective People: Powerful Lessons in Personal Change.* Simon and Schuster, 1989.

5. Dawkins, Richard. *The Selfish Gene* (30th Anniversary Edition). Oxford University Press, 1976 (2006).

6. Eisler, Riane. The Chalice & The Blade: *Our History. Our Future.* Harper Collins, 1987.

7. Heilbrun, Carolyn G. *The Last Gift of Time: Life Beyond Sixty.* Ballantine Books, 1997.

8. Hicks, Esther and Jerry. *The Teachings of Abraham, The Vortex: Where the Law of Attraction Assembles All Cooperative Relationships.* Hay House, 2009.

9. Hubbard, Barbara Marx. *52 Codes for Conscious Self Evolution: A Process of Metamorphosis to Realize Our Full Potential Self.* Conscious Evolution, 2010.

10. Hubbard, Barbara Marx. *Conscious Evolution:*

Awakening the Power of Our Social Potential. New World Library, 1998.

11. Kierson, Miles. *Seven Provocations.* CreateSpace, 2011.

12. Laszlo, Ervin. *The Akashic Experience: Science and the Cosmic Memory Field.* Inner Traditions, 2009.

13. Lipton, Bruce H. *The Biology of Belief: Unleashing the Power of Consciousness, Matter and Miracles.* Hay House, 2005.

14. Logan, Dave, John King, Haley Fischer-Wright. *Tribal Leadership: Leveraging Natural Groups to Build a Thriving Organization.* Harper Business, 2011.

15. McNally, Michael D. *Honoring Elders: Aging, Authority, and Ojibwe Religion.* Columbia University Press, 2009.

16. Montagu, Ashley. *The natural superiority of women.* Altamira Press, 1953.

17. Pert, Candace B. *Molecules of Emotion: The Science Behind Mind-Body Medicine.* Scribner, 1997.

18. Pevny, Ron. *Conscious Living: Conscious Aging.* Atria, 2014.

19. Pierce, Joseph Chilton. *Exploring the Crack in the Cosmic Egg: Split Minds and Meta-Realities.* Park Street Press, 2014.

20. Radin, Dean. *The Conscious Universe: The Scientific Truth of Psychic Phenomena.* Harper Edge, 1997.

21. Ram Dass. *Still Here: Embracing Aging, Changing, and Dying*. Riverhead Books, 2000.

22. Rann, Michael C. and Arrott, Elizabeth R. *Shortcut to a Miracle: How to Change Your Consciousness and Transform Your Life*. Jeffers Press, 2005.

23. Russell, Peter. *Waking Up in Time: Finding Inner Peace in Times of Accelerating Change.* Wisdom Media, 1992.

24. Sarton, May. *At Seventy: A Journal.* WW Norton and Company, 1984.

25. Schachter-Shalomi, Zalman and Miller, Ronald S. *From Age-Ing to Sage-Ing: A Revolutionary Approach to Growing Older.* Hachette Book Group, 1995.

26. Talbot, Michael. *The Holographic Universe.* Harper Collins, 1991.

27. Teilhard de Chardin, Pierre. *The Phenomenon of Man.* Harper Perennial Classics, reprint 2008.

28. Thomas, William H. *Second Wind: Navigating the Passage to a Slower, Deeper and More Connected Life.* Simon and Schuster, 2014.

29. Thomas, William H. *In The Arms of Elders: A Parable of Wise Leadership and Community Building.* Vander Wyck and Burnham, 2006.

30. Thomas, William H. *What Are Old People For? How Elders Will Save the World.* Vander Wyck and Burnham, 2004.

31. Twist, Lynne. *The Soul of Money: Reclaiming the Wealth of Our Inner Resources.* WW Norton and Company, 2003.

32. Zaffron, Steve and Dave Logan. *The Three Laws of Performance: Rewriting the Future of Your Organization and Your Life.* Jossey-Bass, 2009.

33. Zeller, Ron. *Aging or Ageless: Rise Like Phoenix from the Myth of Aging.* CreateSpace, 2014.

Appendix 1: The Role of the Aged

For this discussion, the *aged* are defined as those old people who are physically and/or mentally incapacitated and incapable of providing self-care.

The aged play a role of great service to the community. As pointed out by Dr. William H. Thomas in his parable *In the Arms of Elders,* the aged create the soul of community. In their infirmity, they provide the gift of allowing the community to come together in their care. As recipients, they are the gift itself. In that interaction they become the glue of community, the bond of community.

Dr. Thomas has proposed that the community is responsible for relieving the three plagues of the aged: helplessness, loneliness, and boredom. It is not the medicine of the scientist that our aged require, but rather the medicine of the compassionate community. And the community serves itself by serving their aged. The aged could be considered the very source of community. Their care bonds us.

Humans are the only species that takes care of its aged. In all other species, those who wear out simply die. Only humans take care of those who can no longer do the physical or mental work of being Adult. Humans are set apart from all other species, not just because of our brain power, not just because of our opposable thumb, but because our grandmothers give care to us and we, in turn, care for our elderly.

We have a natural bond that is so built-in it feels natural for us to take care of each other. The bond remains, even with those of us who are aged. Such goodness in being a human being may well be an expression of our Godness.

Appendix 2: Curriculum Vitae

Born December 6, 1935

Married – Ellen Tolliver

Nine children.

Educational Background

University of Massachusetts: 1953-1957, B.S. Degree

Albany Medical College: 1957-1961, M.D. Degree

Surgical Intern: Albany Medical Center Hospital, 1961-1962

Surgical Training

General Surgery

Albany Medical Center Hospital, Albany, NY: 1962-1963

U.S.A.F., Lockbourne A.F.B., Ohio: 1963-1965

Methodist Hospital, Dallas, TX (Chief Resident): 1965-1966

Plastic Surgery

Allegheny General Hospital, Pittsburgh, PA: 1966-1967

Western Pennsylvania Hospital, Pittsburgh, PA: 1967-1968

Board Certified

American Board of Plastic and Reconstructive Surgery, 1970

Membership

American Society of Plastic Surgeons

Virginia Society of Plastic Surgery

American Medical Association

Licensure

Delaware, Active. Virginia, Inactive.

Practice

1968-1977: Pittsburgh, PA – Private practice of Plastic and Reconstructive Surgery

Chief of Plastic Surgery at St. Francis Hospital, Suburban

General Hospital and St. Margaret's Hospital. Surgical staff Passavant and West Pennsylvania Hospitals.

1978 - January 2004: Founder and Senior Surgeon of The Austin-Weston Center for Cosmetic Surgery, Reston, Virginia. Four Board-Certified Plastic surgeons and 35 staff.

Teaching Appointments

University teaching appointment at Albany Medical College during residency training.

Teaching faculty at St. Francis General Hospital: Surgical Residency Training Program

Teaching faculty at Western Pennsylvania Hospital: Plastic Surgery Residency Training Program

Lecturer, Walter Reed Hospital and Georgetown University

Medical Articles and Presentations: 1990-2005

June 2005: Presentations, Faculty, Nordic Course, International Society of Aesthetic Plastic Surgery, Stockholm, Sweden "Rejuvenating the Older Face" and "Melissa: The Story of Transformation."

May 2004: Presentations, Faculty, International Society of European Plastic Surgery, Ghent Belgium, "The Aging Mouth," "The Older Aging Face," Panel Participant on Bioethics in Plastic Surgery, presenting "Melissa: The Ideal Cosmetic Surgical Candidate."

April 2004: Presentations, Albany Medical College, Physician's Bioethics, "The Death of Donald," Bioethics in Plastic Surgery, presenting "Melissa": the Ideal Cosmetic Surgical Candidate."

April 2004: Presentations, Faculty, Brazilian Society of Plastic Surgery, Sao Paulo, Brazil, "The Aging

Mouth." "The Older Aging Face," Panel Participant on Bioethics in Plastic Surgery, presenting "Melissa: The Ideal Cosmetic Surgical Candidate."

October 2003:, Lead-Off Address, "The Death of Donald" Inova Hospital System, Physician's Bioethical Conference, Caring for the Patient at the End of Life. 2003 "Surgical Treatment of the Aging Mouth," Seminars in Plastic Surgery, Volume 17, Number 2. With Poindexter, B; Sigal, R; Weston, G.

May 2003: Presentations, Faculty, International Society of Aesthetic Plastic Surgery, Mexico City, Mexico, "The Transtemple Lift" and "The Saggy Mouth Corner."

November 2002: "Cosmetic Surgery Reveals," Editorial, *Journal of Plastic and Reconstructive Surgery.*

July 2002: Presentation to the Baja Plastic Surgery Society, Faculty, Tijuana, Mexico, "Surgical Treatment of the Aging Mouth."

November 2002: Teaching Course, American Society of Plastic Surgery, "Surgical System for the AgED Face."

Winter 2001: "Outpatient Surgery in the Office Surgical Facility," *Fairfax County Medical Society NEWS.*

November 2001: Teaching Course, American Society of Plastic Surgery, "Surgical System for the AgED Face."

2000: "Rejuvenating the Aged Face." *Perspectives in Plastic Surgery,* with Sigal, R, Weston, G and Poindexter, B, vol. 14, no. 2, 2000.

1996-1998: Series of columns about Cosmetic Surgery, published in advertisement form in *The Washington Post Magazine, Architectural Digest, The Washingtonian Magazine* and *Town and Country Magazine*.

1994: "Rejuvenating the Aging Mouth," *Perspectives in Plastic Surgery,* vol. 8, no. 1, pp. 27-56, 1994.

October 1992: "Facelift Tips," *The Technical Forum.*

August 1992: The Clinics of Plastic Surgery article was quoted extensively in *Plastic Surgery Outlook*, vol. 6, no. 6.

April 1992: Quoted in Letter to the Editor from Alfred E. Greenwald, M.D., *Plastic and Reconstructive,* Surgery 89, Number 4.

April 1992: Publication, *Virginia Medical Quarterly,* "Cosmetic Surgery of the Aging Mouth," 118:110-111, April 91.

April 1992: Publication of chapter in *Clinics of Plastic Surgery,* "Rejuvenation of the Aging Mouth," with Weston, G., Saunders.

August 1991: Quoted in *Technical Forum.*

July 1991: Presentation of "Rejuvenation of the Aging Mouth," International Cosmetic Surgery Meeting, Beverly Hills, California. ("Adrian Aiache Course")

June 1991: Presentation of "The Corner Lift," Ohio Valley Society of Plastic and Reconstructive Surgery.

January 1991: Presentation "Augmentation of the Mid-Face with RTV Silicone," presented at the Virgin Island Conference of Plastic Surgery, Tortola, BVI.

January 1991 Presentation of "Rethinking the Basic Face Lift," presented at the Virgin Island Conference of Plastic Surgery, Tortola, BVI.

December 1990: Presentation, Anne Arundel Dental Society. "The Importance of Lips in Cosmetic Dentistry."

June 1990: Publication of the leading article in the *Journal of the American Medical Writers Association,* "The Collaborative Model Signifies a Patient-Physician Relationship: The Pairing of Equals." Vol 5;2, June, 1990.

1965-1990: Approximately 20 scientific presentations and publications, including the National Chief Resident's Award in 1968 for Best Paper, "Basal Cell Nevus Syndrome" and co-author of chapter, "The Vagal Body Tumor."

Personal Development Trainings

The following list includes forty-five participatory programs – trainings, retreats, and workshops – representing thousands of hours of inquiry, self-discovery, and reorientation. These have served as Elder Training par excellence.

During these courses, participants examined some of the big questions: *Who am I? Where am I? What am I doing here? What is life all about? Where are our world trends taking us? Can humanity co-create its own evolutionary process?*

Landmark Worldwide Programs

The *est* Training

Seminars (6)

Wisdom Course 1, 2, and 3

Leadership Courses

The Landmark Forum (reviewed x 3)

The Advanced Course (reviewed)

Communication Courses (4)

Heart-Based Work

Year-long course led by psychologist Elaine Weiner

Temenos Workshop (and subsequent programs below)

Men's Gathering (5 days)

Opening the Heart Workshop (10 days residential)

Pathways I Program (10 days residential)

Pathways II Program – Investigating the Dark Side (10 days residential)

Pathways III Program – Opening the Third Eye (10 days residential)

Temenos Mystery School (3 years)

And More

Dream Analysis – Jungian Analyst Julie Bondanza (4 years)

The Hoffman Quadrinity Process (8 days residential)

Re-birthing Program of Leonard Orr with Eugenie Starr

Miracle of Love (10 days residential)

Vision Fast with Lynnaea Lumbard and Rick Paine (11 days in the desert)

Workshops with Elisabeth Kübler-Ross, Michael Harner, Neale Donald Walsch, Don Miguel Ruiz, Jon Kabat-Zinn, Raymond Moody, Brian Weiss

Loving Relationship Training with Sondra Ray

Past Life Regressions (3)

Enneagram Training

Challenge Day Workshop

Agent of Conscious Evolution with Barbara Marx Hubbard (1 year)

Founder, Archimedes Writing Group

Investor Trips (4) to villages in Senegal, India, Burkina Faso, and Bangladesh (The Hunger Project).

Appendix 3: The Facts of Epee

There are four areas of critical concern in the world today: Energy, Population, Environment, and Economics. Since an epee (eh′ pay) is a thin light sword that bends easily, EPEE serves as a useful metaphor. The world's EPEE has bent to its limits, and it is about to snap.

Energy Facts

Our fossil fuels are running out. Fracking and natural gas production are like drinking the dregs, more and more expensive dregs.

Oil company executives base the investment value of their companies on the fossil fuels *still underground.* They plan to continue to remove and sell the fuels, regardless of the consequences to our atmosphere.

The use of alternate sources of energy such as wind, sun, or tides is expanding, but these may not replace fossil fuels fast enough.

China and India plan to continue their industrial expansion, and their demands for additional resources are insistent.

Population Facts

For thousands of generations, the world population was stable at less than a billion. Over a mere eight generations (1815 to 2015), our population has leaped 800 percent to 7. 3 billion humans. Populations of the poorest nations continues to swell.

Environmental Facts

- The oceans cover seventy-one percent of the Earth's surface and contains ninety-seven percent of the planet's water.
- The temperature of the sea is rising and it is becoming more acidic.
- Greenhouse gases are the highest they have been in 300,000 years.
- Glaciers store about sixty-nine percent of Earth's fresh water as ice. They are retreating.
- Ninety percent of the world's ice is stored in the Antarctic ice sheet. It is melting.
- Our world fisheries are either played out or are playing out.
- Certain mighty rivers now scarcely touch their seas – the Indus, the Nile, the Colorado.
- We are losing species at a rate too rapid to be due to natural selection.
- Honeybees are disappearing. Without them there will be no pollination, no food plants.
- Virgin forests are being destroyed at the rate of 200,000 acres per day.
- Global farmland is overworked.

Economic Facts

- Our current capitalist economy is interest-based and corporations pay off investors with the money from new investors. Ponzi schemes collapse, leaving all holding the empty bag.
- Corporations have the same benefits as citizens but without their restraints.
- Our interest system, whereby you must return $106 when you borrow $100, requires a constant increase in production and a constant acceleration in the rate resource use. We only have one Earth but, to keep up production, we are using up the resources of almost two Earths.
- Forty percent of our human brothers and sisters live on less than $4 per day.
- The gap between the wealthiest ten percent and the poorest ten percent is widening.
- Some economists proclaim we are fine. Others, looking from a larger view, say things like: "Our economic system is hanging by a thread" and "We face a global economic collapse within our lifetimes."

These Three Facts Leap Out

1. It takes the resources of almost TWO Earths to support our present world's lifestyle.
2. If our entire world lived as we do in the United States, it would take over FOUR Earths to sustain us.
3. We have only ONE Earth. – Global Footprint Network.

Appendix 4: The Five Stages of Grief

The five stages of grief include:

1. **Denial** – Because the reality of loss is hard to face, one of the first reactions is Denial. We try to shut out the reality or magnitude of the situation, and begin to develop a false, preferable reality.

2. **Anger** – After Denial comes Anger, the *Why Me* stage. There are misplaced feelings of rage and envy. Anger can manifest itself in different ways. People can be angry with themselves or with others, especially those close to them. It is important to remain detached and nonjudgmental when dealing with a person experiencing Anger from grief.

3. **Bargaining** – The third stage involves the hope that we can somehow undo or avoid the source of our grief. For example, "Can we still be friends?" when facing a break-up. We may use anything valuable as a bargaining chip as we seek to negotiate a compromise. We might bargain with a higher power, "If you bring them back, I promise I will ..." (fill in the blank). Bargaining rarely provides a sustainable solution, especially if it is a matter of life or death.

4. **Depression** – During the fourth stage, we begin to understand loss and the certainty of death. We may address the existential concept of the void, adopting the idea that living is pointless. Things begin to lose meaning. Because of this, we may become silent, refuse to socialize, and spend much time crying and being sullen.

This process allows the grieving person to disconnect from love and affection, possibly in an attempt to avoid further trauma.

Depression is like a dress rehearsal for the aftermath. It is a kind of acceptance with emotional attachment. It is natural to feel sadness, regret, fear, and uncertainty when going through this stage. Feeling those emotions shows we have begun to accept the situation.

5. **Acceptance** – In this last stage, we begin to come to terms with mortality, of ourselves or a loved one, or we acknowledge the reality of a tragic event. This stage varies with the situation. Someone who is dying may reach Acceptance before the people they will leave behind.

Acceptance typically comes with a calm, retrospective view and a stable mindset.

Elisabeth Kübler-Ross originally developed this model for the stages of grief based on her observations of people suffering from terminal illness. She later expanded her theory to apply to any form of catastrophe.

Kübler-Ross stated that these stages do not necessarily come in order, nor are all stages experienced by all individuals. She claimed a person will experience at least two of the stages. Often, people experience several stages in a roller coaster effect, switching between two or more stages, returning to one or more several times before working through it. Women are more likely than men to experience all five stages.

However, the Kübler-Ross hypothesis states that there are individuals who struggle with death until the end. Some psychologists believe the harder a person fights death, the more likely they will remain in the denial stage. If this is the case, it is possible a person will have more difficulty dying in a dignified way.

Appendix 5: Me OR We, You Choose

Inspired by Archangel Uriel, World Teacher, Received and Messaged by Phillip Elton Collins, The Angel News Network:

Dear Divine Human Souls,

It is the destiny of your planet and humanity to move from a "me" consciousness to a "we" consciousness. Let us examine the two forms of consciousness and through your discernment and freedom of will and choice, decide what resonates for you. Which do you wish to be?

ME Consciousness

This is a way of feeling and thinking that you are individuals who are responsible for your own achievements. There is little true intimacy or compassion for or with others. There is little connection to higher realms from whence you came, and love and support you now.

The ways and means to support your human reality/existence are: (1) Materialism/Social Status, (2) Power/Control (few controlling the many), (3) Accumulations of monetary wealth, and (4) Imbalanced focus with the self.

The mental body housing the ego is powered by (1) Fear, (2) Narcissism/Arrogance, (3) Doubt, (4) Ignorance, (5) Resentment/Rage, and (6) Lack of self-love, thus others.

Most truth is hidden and knowledge and wisdom (applied knowledge) are replaced for validation and profit often through deceit and denial of the deceit.

WE Consciousness

Through applied knowledge (wisdom) it is understood that you are all connected and integrated and are here to support and love one another in creating communities of equality, harmony and balance.

There is a constant readiness and commitment to support the purpose of each of you being here (soul plan) through a balance of giving and receiving and the balance of the masculine and feminine energies. There is an innate knowing there is a limitless supply for all.

Truth reigns supreme. There is neither deceit nor denial of the deceit. All information/communication is authentic and transparent. You all know the same thing at the same time.

The world is filled with heartfelt intentions, not just ego satisfaction; you are learning to 'think' with your knowing/loving hearts, not just your minds.

The sacred journey of each individual is recognized, honored and valued as an essential aspect of the whole of humanity.

Love is known and seen as the powerhouse of all reality, thus seen in all things (plants, animals, minerals, air, water, and the seen and unseen).

Learning how to heal individual wounds and defenses is being mastered, allowing unconditional love, supporting each one's highest good is being achieved.

In Conclusion

Which consciousness resonates for you? Once you choose one, fully embrace it in your individual life and radiate it out to others. Be prepared for the responsibilities and consequences of each choice. One of these contains a higher vibration than the other which will allow the other to entrain to the other. Are you ready to create a new world paradigm? The formula is here, if you so choose to apply it.

Appendix 6: A Conversation with God

I once spent a long weekend at Omega Institute in a training with Neale Donald Walsch, author of *Conversations with God.* He was there with his wife, Em, a poet. Neale talked and Em read poems to the group.

When the weekend goal was upon us, it was time for us to speak with God. Neale had been assuring us that God would speak back.

"Write down your question for God," he told us.

My question had been troubling me for years. So I wrote:

God, if you were to replace each of us healthy American adults sitting in these chairs with a hunger-bellied child from the lands of starvation, each child being one of those 10,000 of your children dying daily of starvation, and if each were to die within a few days, and you gazed upon these, your dying children, what would you say to them?

Then Neale told us, "Now write down God's answer."

There was a pause.

Then we understood. Pens dropped to the paper. And my words flowed forth:

I greet you, my darling children. Thank you for being here with me. I salute you for having chosen to make your particular journey. Thank you for being the ones to have come in these times. Because of you, there will be an end to hunger and starvation. Remember, it was you who said this is what you came for, my courageous ones. I love you. I shall see you soon.

From this life-altering experience with Neale and Em and God, I understood I could have a conversation with God at any time on any topic.

While this was my own particular experience, you may have a conversation with God yourself. Perhaps you will discover you birthed yourself at this particular time for the purpose of becoming an Elder in this critical era for our human species. You are not just the actor, but also the director and producer of the magnificent and unique play called "My Life."

Appendix 7: Young Child as Elder

There is no particular age when one becomes an Elder. Occasionally, an individual may begin to demonstrate the qualities of compassion, straightforwardness, and kindness, Elder traits all, at a young age. Usually such children are mocked, called "little old men" or "little old women."

A child who speaks wisdom typically will be put in his or her place. Parents and Adult friends may diminish with comments like: "Aw, how cute is that?" or "Out of the mouths of babes."

It is difficult for any parent to accept the idea that their young child might be more mature, more grown-up, and more Elder than they are.

As Wordsworth said, "Shades of the counting-house close round the growing boy."

I would often sit with my youngest daughter, Brittany, as she fell asleep. One evening when she was around five years old, I sat with her. She was half asleep, using her baby blanket to stroke her cheek. Then she brightened for a moment and said, "Everyone lives a different section of life."

Cool, I thought; I didn't even know she knew the word *section.*

"And no two people live the same section." She paused. "And there are more sections of life than there are people who've lived them."

I was astonished. "Where did you get that?"

“I made it up,” she replied in a smug voice.

Now she had my full attention. Almost asleep, hand still stroking her cheek with the corner of her blankie, she was quiet. Her eyes were closed.

Mine were wide open.

She said, “You don’t need to *have* a reason to be here.”

I thought she was talking about me, but she wasn’t.

“Nope. You don’t have to have a reason.” She paused. “But on the other hand ... if you *gotta* have a reason....” Her eyes opened and she grinned at me. “Then be my guest.”

“Where did you get *that*?”

“Made that up, too.”

She closed her eyes and fell asleep.

It took me a while to fall asleep that night. I lay in bed, wondering who this little person I had adopted *really* was.

Appendix 8: The Small Town Saga of Dr. Elder and Dr. Adult

Dr. Elder decided he would open up a practice in the small town to which he had recently retired. He put up a sign:

DR. ELDER'S CLINIC

All treatments $500

$1000 back if not cured.

Dr. Adult, the other doctor in town, was certain the old man knew little about practicing modern-day medicine, so he thought he had an opportunity to make an easy $1000. Disguised, he went to Dr. Elder's clinic.

Dr. Adult: I have lost all taste in my mouth. Can you please help me?

Dr. Elder: Nurse, please bring the medicine from box 22 and put 3 drops on this man's tongue.

Dr. Adult: Aaargh! That's gasoline!

Dr. Elder: Congratulations! You have your taste back. That will be $500.

Dr. Adult was annoyed, so he left the clinic. He returned a few days later, however, after figuring out a way to recover his money.

Dr. Adult: I have lost my memory, I cannot remember anything.

Dr. Elder: Nurse, bring the medicine from box 22 and put 3 drops on this man's tongue.

Dr. Adult: Oh no you don't – that's gasoline!

Dr. Elder: Congratulations! You have your memory back. That will be $500.

Dr. Adult, now $1000 poorer, left the clinic, angrily. He returned a few days later with a new plan.

Dr. Adult: My eyesight has become weak. I can hardly see.

Dr. Elder: Well, I don't have any treatment for that. Here's your $1000 back.

Dr. Adult: But this is only $500.

Dr. Elder: Congratulations! You have your vision back! That will be $500.

The lesson in this little story is: Don't think by being an Adult you can outsmart an Elder. Life just doesn't work that way.

Index

A

B

C

D

E

F

G

H

I

J

K

L

M

N

O

P

Q

R

S